Rare WORDS II

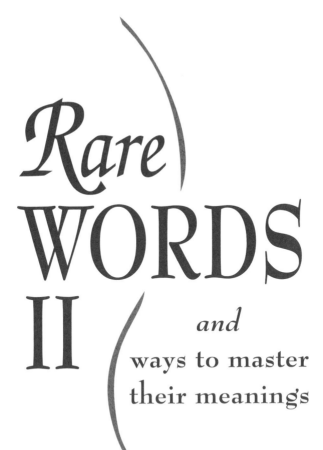

Rare WORDS II

and
ways to master their meanings

500 MORE
UNUSUAL SELECTIONS,
SOME WITH
POETIC CONFECTIONS
FOR GLEANING
THEIR MEANING

Jan Leighton   Hallie Leighton

Illustrations by Marina de Conciliis

LEVENGER
PRESS

Published by
Levenger Press
420 South Congress Avenue
Delray Beach, Florida 33445-4696
Levengerpress.com

First Edition

  Library of Congress Cataloging-in-Publication Data

Leighton, Jan, 1921-
  Rare words II and ways to master their meanings : 500 more unusual
selections, some with poetic confections for gleaning their meaning / Jan
Leighton, Hallie Leighton ; illustrations by Marina de Conciliis. -- 1st ed.
     p. cm.
  Sequel to: Rare words, 2003.
  Includes bibliographical references and index.
  ISBN 978-1-929154-31-9
  1. Vocabulary. I. Leighton, Hallie, 1970- II. Conciliis, Marina de,
1970-ill. III. Title.
  PE1449.L3663 2008
  428.1--dc22
                                    2007046338

Cover and book design by Danielle Furci
Illustrations by Marina de Conciliis
www.marinadeconciliis.com
Mim Harrison, Editor

To Lynda Myles and James Pendleton

But words are things, and a small drop of ink,
Falling like dew, upon a thought, produces
That which makes thousands, perhaps millions, think.

—Lord Byron, *Don Juan,* 1819

Contents

Introductions

"Words, words, mere words," sighed Shakespeare's disillusioned Troilus, as he tore up a letter from his inconstant lover, Cressida.

It's a shame he didn't have this book.

These words are not *mere* words. We have mined the English language for 500 more lovely rarities, from **abulia** to **yare**, words whose very look and sound herald their distinction. A well-turned word can turn a word-lover's head. In selecting these rarities, we have gone above and beyond the call of beauty, finding words that are truly useful as well. The word **gravid** is pregnant with meaning. A word like **athanasia** deserves to be immortalized. **Redound** redounds to the credit of anyone who uses it.

What's more, these words have histories and pasts. And they'll take you places.

More years ago than I care to count, I studied acting at the American Theater Wing, in a class whose students included Colleen Dewhurst and Bob Fosse. Once, I was performing a scene in Sophie Treadwell's *Machinal* that required me to remove my shirt. My teacher, the late, great actor and director Joe Anthony, took this occasion to tell the class a story about the **ka** in ancient Egypt, a spirit that resided in a statue after a person's death, and that represented its owner in an idealized state of youth, vigor and beauty.

I think he was **chaffing** me for the pride that he sensed I took in my toned physique. But I **vail** my hat to Joe Anthony for introducing this fascinating word to the class (not to mention comparing me to an Egyptian statue). Whenever I run across ka in a crossword or conversation, I think of the Egyptian pyramids—and Joe Anthony. For me, a little of the ka of Joe Anthony resides in that word.

Introductions

Egypt is just one of the lands to which this slim little volume will take you: cyrenaic lands us in neighboring Libya. The word refers to an ancient Greek school of philosophy founded by a fellow named Aristippus, who held that pleasure is the only rational aim in life. His philosophy sounds reasonable, but wherefore the name? Because Aristippus hailed from Cyrene, an ancient Greek colony in Libya.

Now let's fly over the wadis of the Middle East and cross the Mediterranean to disembark in Lydia, an ancient kingdom known for its dulcet melodies. This eponym of Lydian, a musical mode, is located in what is now Turkey, not far from where poor Troilus tore up Cressida's letter.

On the subject of music and lovers, let's chassé over to *charivari*, a cacophonous kettle-banging serenade used to mock newlyweds in an unpopular marriage. French settlers carried the tradition to New Orleans, where it was re-christened a shivaree, now performed more in fun than derision.

Already we have traversed four continents, and we've covered only a handful of words. There are hundreds more herein, each with its own splendid history that enriches its meaning. I hope that you enjoy these words as much as we have enjoyed compiling them, and that each one opens up a new world for you.

—Jan Leighton

When my dad approached me about writing a sequel to *Rare Words*, I was hesitant. I thought we had collected all the rare but useful words left in the English language in our first book. Where would we find 500 more rarities as interesting as the first?

To my surprise, Dad had already collected them. Where had these words been hiding? There were

Introductions

hundreds and hundreds more unfamiliar but fascinating words out there that deserved broader use.

For example, a melisma is the squeezing of many notes into one sung syllable, a prevalent vocal style in many popular music genres today. To crizzle is to acquire a rough, crumpled look on the surface, as water does before it freezes. Dad had assembled the gems, and once again my job was to display them and, with my dad, devise mnemonics to help readers remember them, just as we had with the original *Rare Words*.

But for this sequel, Dad and I were not satisfied with repeating a winning formula. So we developed a new mnemonic form that I dubbed the rarihew. The rarihew is an adaptation of the clerihew, a verse form named after Edmund Clerihew Bentley (1875-1956), an Englishman who invented and wrote a book full of them. Here is one:

> John Stuart Mill,
> By a mighty effort of will,
> Overcame his natural bonhomie
> And wrote 'Principles of Economy.'

If one were to write a verse about Mr. Bentley, it could go like this:

> Bentley, Edmund Clerihew
> was someone merry who
> mocked men in a terse
> irregular form of verse.

Like the clerihew, the rarihew is humorous and has irregular meter; unlike the clerihew, the rarihew has as its subject a rare word rather than a person. Its purpose is to help the reader remember the word.

Most of our rarihews follow the traditional clerihew rhyme pattern (AABB, with the subject of the verse ending the first line). We did not, however, always adhere strictly to the form. Some verses worked better in ABAB format; a couple have three or five lines rather than four. (That's one of the benefits of making up a new form: you don't always have to stick to it.) In most cases, the rare word ends the line to form one of the rhymes, to make it easier to memorize.

In addition to Edmund Clerihew Bentley, another source of our poetic inspiration was Ogden Nash, who is famous for his whimsical alterations of words to create rhymes (for example, rhyming "important" with "ortant," a stand-in for "oughtn't"). Many of our rhymes are written with a nod to the Nashian spirit.

That said, every verse was composed to help the reader unlock the meaning of the word. Any attempt to be witty is in the service of this aim. Thus, when forced to decide whether the last verse of the **laches** rarihew should be the more poetic "the law doesn't love the late" or the more specific "you lose your rights if you're late," we chose the latter, because forfeiting rights is essential to understanding what laches means.

We did, however, bend grammar to create rhymes (as do most writers of verse). For example, many of our adjectives are used **postpositively** (after the noun) for the sake of rhyme, even though only one of our words is placed postpositively in prose (**redivivus**).

In words with two or more meanings, our verse illustrates the meaning listed first. The first definition is not always the primary or original definition of the word, but rather, the one we think most interesting. The primary definition of **limpet** is a mollusk found clinging to rocks on beaches. But it is the figurative definition— an official who clings to his or her office—that is more readily applicable in real life (except, perhaps, for marine biologists). That definition appears first (see also **ecdysis** and **flummery**). In general, we find metaphorical meanings of words are often the most useful ones.

Words with two etymologically unrelated meanings have separate entries. We do not, however, exhaustively list all senses of a word. For example, we do not give the

Introductions

biological definition of **meiosis** or the medical definition of **sigmoid**, listing instead the meanings we think will be more useful to a general audience.

Another difference between *Rare Words II* and a dictionary is that the words are not listed alphabetically but somewhat randomly. This is done to ward off what I call *aba-abba-abecedarianism*, the tedium of reading a group of words dictionary-style. (That's not how most of us read dictionaries.) This also enabled us to place related words together.

To satisfy the abecedarian impulse, there is an alphabetical index at the back, as well as an alphabetical category index at the front. And to please crossword and board game buffs, we have included a handful of words that pop up frequently in those games, such as **aa**, **ai**, **oe** and **qat**.

Although *Rare Words II* is not a dictionary, all words save two are in at least one major English-language dictionary. Not one of these dictionaries, however, contains all of our words. (Our list of major English-language dictionaries includes *American Heritage, Merriam-Webster Unabridged,* the *Oxford English Dictionary* and *Random House Unabridged.*) The two words not in any major dictionary are **chresmologue** and **parkour**. Despite its absence from a major dictionary, chresmologue is described in several books and was the subject of an essay by the anthropologist Loren Eiseley. Parkour was the subject of a 2007 *New Yorker* article and will probably appear in the next edition of several dictionaries.

Which reminds me of a promise I made in the introduction to our first book. I said that once you learned those words, they would show up in many places—either because you were now attuned to them or because our book helped to popularize them. (Just last night, I met up with *louche*—a *Rare Words* word—in a play. I felt as if I had run into an old friend.)

Introductions

My hope is that the same thing will happen when you encounter a word from this book. These words are worthy of becoming less rare. Welcome to *Rare Words* redivivus.

—Hallie Leighton

Pronunciation Key and Abbreviations

Pronounced	As in
a	mat
ā or ay	day
ah or o	hot
aw	law or more
b	boy
ch	chin
d	day
e or eh	pet
ee	feed
f or ff	fill
g	go
h	hot
ī	hide
i or ih	kiss or agent
j	joy
k	kitten
l	lad
m	mad
n	not
ng	sing
o	hot
ō	hope
oi	boy
oo	boo
ou	out
p	pan
r	run
s or ss	yes
sh	shine
t	tin
th	thing
th	then
u or uh	run
ur	hurt
v	vote
y	young
z	zoo
zh	beige

Pronunciation Key and Abbreviations

The pronunciation appears in parentheses following each word. Syllables are separated by hyphens. The accented syllable appears in large capital letters, the nonaccented syllables in lower case. In words with two accented syllables, the secondary accent appears in smaller capital letters (e.g., **athanasia**: ATH-uh-NAY-zhuh).

Guide to Abbreviations

adj.	adjective
adv.	adverb
e.g.	for example (Latin: *exempli gratia*)
esp.	especially
etc.	and so forth (Latin: *et cetera*)
n.	noun
n.pl.	noun plural
prep.	preposition
ult. [from]	ultimately [from]†
v.i.	intransitive verb (no direct object— e.g., "I walked")
v.t.	transitive verb (takes a direct object— e.g., "I threw the ball")
v.i., v.t.	verb can be both intransitive and transitive (e.g., "I walked" or "I walked the dog")

† Indicates that one or more steps in a word's etymology have been skipped for brevity's sake. For example, **bayadère**, meaning striped, is from a French word meaning female dancer, which is from the Portugese *bailadeira*, which is from the Portugese *bailar*, to dance, from the Latin *ballare*. One can skip the French and Portugese and say that bayadère is ult. from the Latin *ballare*, to dance.

Alphabetical Listing of Words by Category

Each word appears in its most appropriate category or categories. For example, **olitory** (pertaining to a kitchen garden) appears in both *Food and Drink* and *Grounds and Domicile*.

Words with two or more meanings appear in each applicable category. For example, **pestiferous** appears in both *Body and Medicine* (as in bringing disease) and *Traits and Activities, Negative* (as in pernicious).

Categories

Artifacts and Omens

Arts and Architecture

Body and Medicine

Food and Drink

Grounds and Domicile

Imagination and Emotions

Language and Speech

Law and Order

Learning and Knowledge

Life and Death

Manners and Mores

Movement and Time

Nature and Matter

Order and Disorder

Place and Relation

Plants and Animals

Politics and Finance

Quantity and Measure

Romance and Sexuality

Shape and Color

Sight and Sound

Spirituality and Belief

Style and Dress

Texture and Smell

Traits and Activities, Negative

Traits and Activities, Positive and Neutral

Words by Category

Artifacts and Omens

ambsace	23
apotropaic	97
bibelot	18
chresmologue	56
comminate	70
dido	17
dunnage	93
echt	108
ensorcell	70
ewer	16
fatidic	45
favonian	33
gadroon	78
handsel	36
imprecate	35
impresa	69
kerf	89
malefic	97
mantic	45
mattock	83
philtre	23
pyx	91
scrutoire	76
sematic	86
shim	93
sortilege	70
theodolite	56
touchstone	51

Arts and Architecture

ashlar	89
bandelet	86
brattice	34
cabotinage	87
chassé	59
cloche	72
Corydon	43
crocket	105
dithyrambic	43
docent	77
hieratic	86
imbricate	55
impasto	85
mullion	34
oubliette	58
picaresque	48
scagliola	85
scumble	72
scupper	92
sough	96
stipple	72
tesselate	14
transom	34
verism	40
vernissage	85
wainscot	89

Body and Medicine

agenesic	48
algesia	76
analeptic	75
anodyne	100
asthenic	76
auscultation	59
barbate	55
buccal	55
cerumen	20
chevelure	74
chine	47
cicatrize	54
climacteric	64
contuse	24
crapulent	28
cyrenaic	13
diathesis	71
encephalon	74
enteron	76
epicene	94
eruct	48
facies	15
febricity	80
foramen	41

Words by Category

Words by Category

Words by Category

Learning and Knowledge

Life and Death

Manners and Mores

Movement and Time

Words by Category

quondam	75		oe	99
saccadic	100		perigee	19
sessile	79		pratal	53
slue	108		putamen	42
spatiate	91		regulus	14
stasis	101		reliquiae	53
tropism	101		riparian	30
ultimo	108		rupicolous	51
vail	104		saprogenic	54
			selenian	20

Nature and Matter

aa	78		sidereal	20
aeolian	30		skift	33
agravic	73		stramineous	47
apogee	19		sylvatic	43
autochthonous	103		thalassic	99
benthos	99		vug	51
bosky	53		wadi	104

Order and Disorder

brontophobia	32		colligate	24
coprolite	52		concatenation	91
cosmogony	30		farrago	63
crizzle	19		perforce	98
dross	29		ravelment	67
drumlin	18		subsume	24
eagre	91		titivate	31

Place and Relation

eburnean	41		anfractuous	33
edaphic	53		apogee	19
eruct	48		appose	89
factitious	86		autochthonous	103
favonian	33		complect	27
foramen	41		conterminous	91
gravic	73		decussate	55
haboob	34		eme	16
hydrargyrum	79		furcate	103
ionosphere	31		intercalate	66
lentic	30		mesial	101
lotic	30		omphalos	56
mesic	61		passim	21
monticle	92		perforce	98
montigenous	86		perigee	19
moraine	18			
nephelognosy	32			
obsidian	103			

Words by Category

postpositive	63	panmixia	17
qua	108	premorse	50
rete	102	pullulate	88
stirps	95	qat	104
theodolite	56	repand	50
weltanschauung	24	rhizoid	102
		riparian	30

Plants and Animals

abscission	102	scandent	53
accipitrine	68	seminal	27
ai	61	stramineous	47
annulose	62	sylvatic	43
attar	107	testudinal	80
barton	65	thuriferous	93
benthos	99	tropism	101
bosky	53	tuckahoe	66
chaff	83	ungulate	42
chine	47	ursine	15
crenate	106	viviparous	62
dendritic	62		

Politics and Finance

dissilient	48	apostasy	60
dumbledor	15	cabotage	52
eburnean	41	camarilla	17
ecdysis	95	chrematistics	81
encephalon	74	countermand	54
endysis	95	depute	85
epigamic	20	dispendious	93
farrier	42	douceur	18
farrow	48	dystopia	38
gramineous	78	engagé	37
halieutics	30	handsel	36
hircine	15	Jacobin	39
hirsute	22	luddite	40
jabiru	68	misprision	75
lentic	30	monopsony	76
limacine	67	oniomania	49
limpet	69	ophelimity	81
lotic	30	prebend	82
lycanthrope	55	princeps	97
malic	24	rapporteur	75
murine	15	regulus	14
ophiolatry	26	relegable	98
oscine	67	samizdat	73

Words by Category

Words by Category

benison	81
Brahman	97
cacodoxy	82
cosmogony	30
discalced	60
ephectic	41
epoche	42
halidom	23
ka	45
laicity	65
luddite	40
monolatry	26
ophiolatry	26
prebend	82
precant	65
salvific	64
sectary	70
seraphic	23
syncretism	40
tergiversate	18
theandric	45
unregenerate	37
vestal	22
viaticum	62

Style and Dress

anadem	29
bayadère	46
bedizen	29
brassard	46
cache-peigne	73
cheviot	46
cloche	72
dido	17
discalced	60
donnish	39
gadroon	78
habiliments	29
mullet	74
scapular	80
titivate	31

Texture and Smell

attar	107
claggy	47
coriaceous	71
fetor	106
grume	47
intactible	69
lubric	24
ozostomia	106
pobby	61
sclerous	41
thuriferous	93

Traits and Activities, Negative

abulia	18
acrasial	20
coffle	58
crapulent	28
desipience	69
diathesis	71
discomfit	63
dragoon	83
dross	29
dyspeptic	25
dysphoria	97
fabulist	22
feckless	19
flagitious	96
fleer	95
fordo	40
froward	37
haver	61
icarian	35
illusor	41
Jacobin	39
jejune	61
limpet	69
maculate	50
malefic	97

Words by Category

miche	40	dulcify	90
mountebank	46	engagé	37
nocent	70	fabulist	22
oniomania	49	farrier	42
onychophagy	49	fillip	49
peccant	60	fugle	45
pestiferous	40	funambulist	44
pococurante	22	gambol	79
prescind	58	guerdon	77
quidnunc	61	irrefragable	89
raffish	21	larky	28
relegable	98	leeftail	52
restive	98	lepid	69
rodomontade	25	ligature	102
saltimbanco	47	lippen	89
scupper	92	moil	31
scutwork	31	nephalist	28
splenetic	98	parkour	68
surd	73	planish	29
sweal	69	premiate	77
trichotillomania	49	prescind	58
trumpery	29	promethean	35
unregenerate	37	pronate	60
yisser	60	propense	100
		pudency	13

Traits and Activities, Positive and Neutral

		puissant	73
		pullulate	88
abscission	102	repine	86
anodyne	100	roister	28
bel esprit	35	sanative	77
blithen	78	scandent	53
brattle	34	scrabble	98
char-work	36	seemly	88
chevy	68	selcouth	43
conation	19	servitor	36
countermand	54	traceur	68
dégagé	37	vendition	52
depute	85	verecund	13
dido	17	vestal	22
dissilient	48	wayworn	99
		yare	106

Rare WORDS II

redivivus (reh-dih-VĪ-vus)

adj. revived; brought back to life (always placed after the noun it modifies; from the Latin, "renewed").

> No man alive is
> a Julius redivivus.
> Of posers, there's plenty.
> New Caesars? Not any.

athanasia (ATH-uh-NAY-zhuh)

n. immortality.

> Princess Anastasia,
> lacking athanasia,
> left a fake
> in her wake.

inchmeal (INCH-meel)

adv. inch by inch; in small increments; gradually.

pudency (PYOO-den-see)

n. modesty.

> Pudency
> is what rude men see
> as a barrier
> if they don't want to marry her.

verecund (VEHR-ih-kund)

adj. modest; bashful.

> If you think Cunégonde
> was verecund,
> you need to re-read
> Voltaire's *Candide*.

cyrenaic (sihr-uh-NAY-ik)

adj. pertaining to hedonism; belonging to an

13

ancient school of philosophers that believed physical pleasure to be more worthy of pursuit than virtue or knowledge (after Aristippus of Cyrene, who founded of the school in the 4th century B.C.E.).

> The student cyrenaic
> skips problems algebraic,
> and applies himself to pleasure
> as a scholar of serious leisure.

ambagious (am-BAY-juss)

adj. circuitous; roundabout; unnecessarily wordy.

> Ambagious
> means outrageous
> in wordiness—
> more is less.

excursus (iks-KUR-suss)

n. a digression, usually in a narrative or appended to a written work.

> The excursus
> is for those who like digressions, versus
> those with a penchant
> for the trenchant.

tesselate (TESS-ih-lut)

adj. arranged in a mosaic.

tesselate (TESS-ih-lāt)

v.t. to fit pieces together with edges touching; to combine into a mosaic.

regulus (REG-yuh-luss)
reguli (REG-yuh-lī)

n., n.pl. a petty king. Also: the metallic mass that sinks to the bottom of a furnace during smelting (from the Latin, "little king"; regulus was the ancient name for antimony because of its ability to combine readily with gold, the king of metals).

Rare WORDS II

ursine (UR-sīn)

adj. pertaining to bears; bear-like.

hircine (HUR-sīn)

adj. resembling a goat or
smelling like a goat.
Also: lustful.

murine (MYUR-īn)

n. a rodent of the genus *Mus. adj.* pertaining to
mice, rats and other rodents of the genus *Mus.*

> The murine makes a beeline
> to avoid the feline;
> in other words, the rat scats
> when it sees the cat.

dumbledor (DUM-bul-dawr)

n. a bumblebee. Also: a scarab beetle.

> In *Harry Potter* lore,
> No one was humbled more
> than Voldemort by Dumbledore.
> Stung by the wizard "bumblebee,"
> Voldemort set his sights on Harry.

facies (FAY-shee-eez)

n. general aspect or outward appearance, as of
the face.

> A woman's facies
> is the way she is
> appearing—
> whether smiling or sneering.

15

prosopagnosia (PRAWS-uh-pag-NŌ-zhyuh)

n. an inability to recognize familiar faces, resulting from a brain disorder that is congenital or stems from injury or disease.

> Even though he knows ya,
> a friend with prosopagnosia
> will fail to recognize
> your face, although he tries.

visile (VIH-zīl)

adj. visually-oriented. *n.* a person who tends to learn visually.

> Though I'm no wiz, I'll
> try to be visile
> and use my eyes
> to memorize.

eme (EEM)

n. a maternal uncle. Also: a friend or close companion.

glossolalia (GLOSS-uh-LAY-lee-uh)

n. meaningless speech uttered in a state of religious ecstasy or trance.

> Glossolalia
> will assail ya
> with words
> that sound absurd.

ewer (YOO-ur)

n. a wide-mouthed pitcher, esp. one with an oval shape, a base and wide spout.

> Ditch your
> old pitcher
> for a ewer
> that's newer.

Rare WORDS II

camarilla (kam-uh-RIH-luh)

n. a group of scheming, private advisors to a person in authority; cabal (from the Spanish; literally, a small chamber, or private cabinet of the king).

exogamy (ek-SAH-guh-mee)

n. marriage outside one's tribe or social unit.

> Hey, guys, don't hog me!
> I prefer exogamy.
> So find me a man
> outside the clan.

endogamy (en-DAH-guh-mee)

n. marriage within one's tribe or social unit.

> New girl, don't dog me.
> I prefer endogamy.
> I'll find a bride
> on the inside.

panmixia (pan-MIK-see-uh)

n. random mating of individuals within a population, any male having an equal likelihood of pairing with any female.

agog (uh-GOG)

adj. highly excited by wonder or anticipation.

> A dog
> is agog
> when you dangle a treat
> of meat.

dido (DĪ-do)

n. a clever trick or prank. Also: a gaudy trinket or bauble.

> To play a dido
> on Fido,
> fake a throw
> and watch him go.

bibelot (BIB-uh-lō)

n. a small curio of rarity or beauty.

douceur (doo-SUR)

n. a tip or bribe.

> "Are you sure
> I should leave a douceur?"
> "Do, Sir.
> A dollar or two, Sir."

moraine (muh-RĀN)

n. an accumulation of mud, soil and stones deposited by a glacier; a landform created by glaciation.

> On arctic terrains
> you'll discover moraines.
> But mud that's glacial
> is no good for a facial.

drumlin (DRUM-lin)

n. an elongated hill or ridge of glacial soil, sand, mud, etc.

tergiversate (tur-JIV-ur-sāt)

v.i. to abandon one's beliefs or repeatedly change one's attitude. Also: to equivocate.

> Tergiversate
> means to equivocate
> or fluctuate
> in views, depending on the news.

abulia (uh-BOO-lee-uh)

n. loss of decision-making ability.

> Some will try to fool ya
> into thinking they've got abulia.
> They'll say their mind is hazy,
> but really, they're just lazy.

conation (kō-NAY-shun)

n. the instinct, urge or desire to act; the drive to exert mental or physical effort.

redound (rih-DOUND)

v.i. to have an effect, for good or ill; to reflect on (e.g., one's honor or reputation).

> I've found
> that good deeds redound
> to one's credit,
> though I wouldn't bet it.

feckless (FEK-liss)

adj. ineffective; incompetent; irresponsible.

> Things feckless
> are "effect-less."
> They have little worth
> on this earth.

crizzle (KRIZ-ul)

v.t., v.i. to become rough on the surface, as water when it starts freezing over; to cause to become rough or irregular on the surface.

perigee (PEHR-ih-jee)

n. the lowest point or least distant position in the orbit of a satellite.

> When the moon is in its perigee,
> Lady Luna is close as she can be
> to Mother Earth,
> for what it's worth.

apogee (AP-uh-jee)

n. the highest point or most distant position in the orbit of a satellite. Also: the summit; highest point (e.g., reached by a culture).

> The biggest gap you see
> between earth and moon
> is when the moon's in apogee
> and you hardly perceive *la lune*.

selenian (sih-LEE-nee-un)

adj. pertaining to the moon.

sidereal (sī-DEER-ee-uhl)

adj. pertaining to the stars.

> Sidereal
> refers to the stars ethereal—
> a nation
> of constellations.

narial (NEHR-ee-ul)

adj. pertaining to the nostrils.

> Any Tom, Dick or Harry will
> trim his tresses narial
> to impress
> someone in a dress.

cerumen (sih-ROO-mun)

n. earwax.

> Cerumen
> requires no groomin'.
> Didn't you hear?
> Swabs can hurt your ear.

acrasial (uh-KRAY-zee-uhl)

adj. pertaining to intemperance or excess; immoderate.

epigamic (ep-i-GAM-ik)

adj. attractive to the opposite sex, as the colors of certain birds are to other birds.

Rare WORDS II

> Could a hammock
> be epigamic?
> Sure, if a girl is impressed
> with her suitor's "love nest."

raffish (RAFF-ish)

adj. vulgar; tawdry; trashy.

> People "giraffe-ish"
> view others as raffish.
> They frown on
> those they look
> down on.

passim (PASS-um)

adv. scattered throughout
(used esp. in bibliographic citations to indicate
that the word or topic being referenced can be
found in various places within the cited source;
from the Latin, "here and there").

onymous (ON-ih-muss)

adj. bearing a name; attributed (the opposite of
anonymous).

> A work signed by Hieronymous
> is onymous;
> a work signed by none of us
> is anonymous.

euonym (YOO-uh-nim)

n. an appropriate name.

> A euonym
> (like "Tiny Tim"
> of *A Christmas Carol* fame)
> is an apt name.

hypocoristic (HĪ-puh-kawr-ISS-tik)

n. a nickname, pet name or diminutive.

> A hypocoristic
> like "Buffy"
> wouldn't stick
> on someone scruffy.

fabulist (FAB-yuh-list)

n. a composer of fables. Also: a liar.

vestal (VESS-tuhl)

adj. chaste; pure (after the virgin priestesses in ancient Rome who maintained the sacred fire of Vesta, the goddess of the hearth). *n.* a virgin woman. Also: a nun.

> A woman vestal
> when put to the test will
> maintain purity
> with great surety.

anchorite (ANG-kuh-rīt)

n. a person living in seclusion for religious reasons; a hermit.

hirsute (HUR-soot)

adj. hairy. Also: covered with stiff hairs or bristles (in botany).

> Hirsute Harry was very cute.
> Although furry, he was no brute.
> His wife, Mary, not being contrary,
> was just wild about her hairy *chérie*.

pococurante (pō-kō-koo-RAN-tee)

n. an indifferent, nonchalant person. *adj.* indifferent and unconcerned.

> You can up the ante,
> but the pococurante
> still doesn't care.
> Now, that's *laissez-faire*.

halidom (HAL-ih-dum)

n. a holy place; sanctuary. Also: something considered holy.

> Folks from both hill and valley come
> to worship at the halidom.
> It's a holy place
> where folks seek grace.

seraphic (sih-RAF-ik)

adj. angelic. Literally: like one of the seraphim, an order of angels.

> In a painting by Vermeer,
> a girl seraphic
> wears a pearl in her ear
> and an expression that could stop traffic.

ambsace (ĀM-zāss)

n. bad luck; something worthless (from the Old French *ambes as*, both aces, the lowest possible throw at dice).

philtre (FIL-tur)

n. a potion believed to have magical power, esp. in arousing sexual desire.

> A potent philtre
> can throw you out of kilter
> and arouse passion
> for one who's not dashin'.

ruttish (RUT-ish)

adj. lustful; salacious.

> One who is ruttish,
> to be rude, is sluttish—
> either a female or male
> whose lust is beyond the pale.

lubric (LOO-brik)

adj. smooth and slippery. Also: lascivious; wanton; lubricious.

malic (MAL-ik)

adj. pertaining to apples or derived from apples.

> A dish both malic
> and Gallic
> is apple *tarte tatin*
> hot off the pan.

contuse (kun-TOOZ)

v.t. to injure without laceration; bruise.

> To contuse
> means to bruise.
> It may hurt like sin,
> but it doesn't break the skin.

subsume (sub-SOOM)

v.t. to bring one principle or idea under the heading or into the category of another, more comprehensive one; to include something specific as part of something general.

colligate (KOL-ih-gāt)

v.t. to group or tie together facts or events, often under a unifying principle or hypothesis.

weltanschauung (VELT-on-SHOU-oong)

n. worldview; an individual or group's viewpoint of the world.

> A weltanschauung
> is a view of the world not short but *lonnng*,
> with a perspective
> that's often collective.

weltschmertz (VELT-shmehrts)

n. mental depression or apathy caused by

comparing reality against an ideal view of the world; worldweariness; sentimental pessimism.

> My weltschmertz
> leaves me so worldweary that it hurts—
> *ja*, I am sad and sentimental,
> so please don't be judgmental.

dyspeptic (diss-PEP-tik)

adj. gloomy; pessimistic.

protreptic (prō-TREP-tik)

n. exhortation; persuasive rhetoric.

> Here's protreptic
> for the dyspeptic:
> Go west, young man, east, south or north.
> Go anywhere, but just go forth!

rodomontade (ROD-uh-mon-TĀD)

n. boasting or bragging; blustery speech. *v.i.* to boast or brag. *adj.* pretentiously boastful (after Rodomonte, a boastful warrior king of Renaissance Italian epics; literally, "one who rolls away the mountain").

> Rodomontade
> is a braggart's tirade,
> and braggarts always boast
> that they know the most.

thrasonic (thruh-SAH-nik)

adj. boasting.

> "No one can beat this mnemonic"
> is a claim thrasonic.
> Is it true?
> I'll leave that up to you.

jactation (jak-TAY-shun)

n. boasting; bragging. Also: restless tossing or twitching.

monolatry (mon-AH-luh-tree)

n. the worship of only one god without denial of the existence of other gods.

> Monolatry
> is not quite idolatry.
> Of gods, you believe in a ton,
> but you worship only one.

ophiolatry (OFF-ee-AWL-uh-tree)

n. the worship of serpents; snake-worship.

> To a practitioner of ophiolatry,
> a snake that falls off a tree
> into the sod
> is a fallen god.

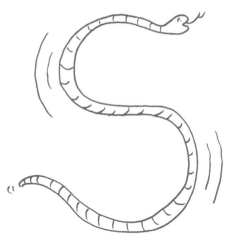

sigmoid (SIG-moid)

adj. s-shaped or c-shaped.

> Imagine what Freud
> could do with *sigmoid*.
> In dreams or awake,
> it's the shape a snake takes.

subulate (SOO-byuh-lit)

adj. thin and tapering to a point, like an awl.

> I had to club you, twit,
> for wielding a tool so subulate.
> Because of horror films and all,
> I am terrified of the awl.

seminal (SEM-ih-nul)

adj. containing the possibility of future development; very influential and original. Originally: pertaining to seed.

complect (kum-PLEKT)

v.t. to weave together; intertwine.

> Things that wind
> up intertwined
> are complected:
> they're interconnected.

banns (BANZ)

n.pl. a public announcement, usually at a church service, of intended marriage.

> The banns
> announce a woman and man's
> decision in life
> to be husband and wife.

shivaree (SHIV-uh-REE)

n. a noisy mock serenade using kettles, pans and other noisemakers for newlyweds, who are sometimes expected to furnish the serenaders with refreshments to quiet them; any raucous mock celebration. *v.t.* to greet with a shivaree.

> A shivaree's
> not chivalry.
> The latter is a knightly code;
> the former a serenade loud and bold
> for a pair newly chosen
> "to have and to hold."

roister (ROY-stur)

v.i. to revel boisterously or noisily. Also: to swagger; be boisterous.

> You can't cloister us
> because we're too boisterous.
> The world is our oyster
> when we roister.

larky (LAHR-kee)

adj. high-spirited; frolicsome; silly.

nephalist (NEF-uh-list)

n. one who completely abstains from alcohol.

> A nephalist
> will insist
> on no alcohol
> at all.

crapulent (KRAP-yuh-lent)

adj. drinking or eating excessively; sick because of drinking too much alcohol.

> A crapulent sap
> should turn off the tap,
> lest this overindulgent gent
> become corpulent.

pursy (PUR-see)

adj. breathing laboriously, esp. from corpulence; shortwinded.

> Coach, please have mercy
> on my son, who is pursy.
> He'll get winded if the timer
> is set too long on the stair climber.

flummery (FLUM-ur-ee)

n. empty compliments; flattery. Literally: a bland custard or pudding, esp. one made of coagulated oatmeal or flour.

habiliments (huh-BIL-ih-mints)

n.pl. clothing or equipment associated with a particular occasion, profession or way of life; trappings.

> The stylish habiliments
> of 19th-century gents
> were crisp white spats
> and black top hats.

bedizen (bih-DĪ-zun)

v.t., v.i. to dress or decorate garishly.

> One who likes to bedizen
> is always accessorizin'
> with items flashy,
> if not quite trashy.

anadem (AN-uh-dem)

n. a wreath worn on the head; a garland.

planish (PLA-nish)

v.t. to smooth (metal) by rolling or hammering.

> The hammer
> creates quite a clamor
> when metal you planish
> to make bumps vanish.

dross (DRAWSS)

n. waste or impure matter, esp. the scum produced by metals during smelting. Also: a worthless or trivial matter.

> Dross
> is stuff that's fit to toss—
> there's no need to stash
> that trash.

trumpery (TRUM-pur-ee)

n. something worthless or trashy; nonsense; rubbish (ult. from the French *tromp*, to deceive).

> Will you throw this trumpery
> in the dump for me?
> I left the junk
> in my trunk.

riparian (rih-PEHR-ee-un)

adj. pertaining to or living on a riverbank.

lotic (LŌ-tik)

adj. pertaining to or living in flowing water.

> Dad's on this boat kick
> observing critters lotic—
> that is, they live in flowing water,
> like the river otter.

lentic (LEN-tik)

adj. pertaining to or living in still water.

> Lentic
> refers to authentic
> denizens of swamps or lakes,
> like many snakes.

halieutics (HAL-ee-OO-tiks)

n. the study of fishing. Also: a treatise on fish or fishing.

aeolian (ee-Ō-lee-un)

adj. windblown or caused by the wind (after Aeolus, the Greek god of the winds).

> Where's a cellar to hold me in?
> There's a storm aeolian
> coming my way.
> *Oy vey!*

cosmogony (koz-MAH-guh-nee)

n. a theory or story of the origin and development of the universe, the solar system or the earth-moon system.

Rare WORDS II

> Anthropologists worldwide agree:
> nearly every culture has a cosmogony—
> a story or myth about Earth's beginning
> or the spark that set the universe spinning.

benighted (bih-NĪ-ted)

adj. intellectually or morally ignorant (literally, overtaken by darkness).

moil (MOIL)

v.i. to work hard. *n.* labor. Also: confusion.

> To moil
> means to toil
> at a desk or in the soil.
> It also means turmoil.

scutwork (SKUT-wurk)

n. tedious work; moil.

> What jerk
> thinks I'd do this scutwork?
> This job I think I'll shirk
> and give myself a caffeinated perk.

titivate (TIT-ih-vāt)

v.t., v.i. to spruce up.

> To titivate
> is to put things in a tidy state
> or make oneself look smart—
> a kind of art.

ionosphere (ī-ON-uh-sfeer)

n. a region of Earth's upper atmosphere, beginning at an altitude of about 35 miles, containing many ionized particles and free electrons, affecting the way radio waves pass through it. Also: a corresponding region above other planets.

nephelognosy (NEF-uh-LOG-nuh-see)

n. scientific observation of clouds.

> Nephelognosy:
> observing the fog you see
> in the sky
> (actually, the clouds that go by).

brontophobia (BRONT-uh-FŌ-bee-uh)

n. abnormal fear of thunder.

> I don't want a phobia
> like brontophobia.
> I'd need a bed to hide under
> every time I heard thunder.

foudroyant (foo-DROY-unt)

adj. striking and stunning in effect, as lightning; dazzling.

> It's as frightening
> as being struck by lightning
> to hear a clairvoyant
> predict something foudroyant.

Rare WORDS II

anfractuous (an-FRAK-choo-us)

adj. full of twisting and turning; sinuous; tortuous.

> Golf courses
> distract us
> with their dog legs anfractuous.

perpend (pur-PEND)

v.t. to consider. *v.i.* to ponder; weigh; deliberate.

> Hamlet, perpending,
> delayed sending
> the evil king to kingdom come,
> but finally he killed the bum.

tautology (taw-TOL-uh-jee)

n. the unnecessary repetition of meaning in different words, such as "free gift"; redundancy. Also: in logic, a compound sentence that is true in all cases, such as "she will or will not go."

orotund (AWR-uh-TUND)

adj. full in sound; sonorous.

> Oratory rotund
> is speech orotund.
> In sound or bombast
> it can't be outclassed.

favonian (fuh-VŌ-nee-un)

adj. pertaining to the west wind, and therefore favorable; gentle; propitious.

> To the Bostonian,
> a Yankees' loss is favonian.
> Then the chance for a Red Sox pennant win
> is more than just a might-have-been.

skift (SKIFT)

n. a light snowfall or rain. Also: a slight trace or touch of something; wisp.

> A skift
> is a light snowfall—
> not enough to form a drift
> or constitute a squall.

haboob (huh-BOOB)

n. a violent sandstorm or dust storm (from the Arabic *habub*, strong wind).

brattle (BRAT-uhl)

n. a clattering or rattling sound. *v.i.* to scamper noisily; make a rattling sound.

> A brattle
> is the sound of a rattle
> so noisy,
> you can hear it in Boise.

brattice (BRAT-iss)

n. a partition erected to conduct air and aid ventilation in a mine.

> I can breathe just fine
> in this mine.
> What a good brattice
> that is!

mullion (MUHL-yun)

n. a strip of wood or stone that divides a window or other opening into smaller panels.

transom (TRAN-sum)

n. a horizontal crossbar dividing a window, or separating a door from the window above it (the phrase "over the transom" refers to the submission of unsolicited manuscripts and evokes images of writers throwing their work through the open window over the door of a publisher's office).

Rare WORDS II

bel esprit (bel-eh-SPREE)
beaux esprits (bō-zeh-SPREE)

n., n.pl. a cultivated, witty person; someone who is intellectually gifted.

> Some are filled with jealousy
> for this bel esprit.
> He's hated
> because he's cultivated.

icarian (ih-KĀR-ee-un)

adj. inadequate for an ambitious project (after Icarus of Greek mythology, who flew too close to the sun with his artificial wings made of wax).

> A word for inadequate is icarian,
> after Icarus, whose wings couldn't carry him
> when he flew too close to the sun.
> They melted, and the poor chap was done.

promethean (pruh-MEE-thee-uhn)

adj. daringly or defiantly creative; boldly original (after Prometheus, the mythical titan who introduced fire to humans).

imprecate (IM-prih-kāt)

v.t., v.i. to curse; invoke evil upon.

> Don't imprecate:
> Don't curse me, Kate!
> I prefer kisses
> to disses.

buss (BUSS)
n. a kiss. *v.t.* to kiss.

singultus (SING-gul-tuss)
n. a hiccup.

> Where did I pick up
> this hiccup?
> I'll not get a single buss
> with this singultus!

char-work (CHAHR-wurk)

n. ordinary manual work such as housework (the same root as charwoman and chore).

servitor (SUR-vih-tur)

n. a servant; attendant.

> Will you have the servitor
> serve it, or
> does service
> make you nervous?

lugent (LOO-jint)

adj. in tears; weeping (from the Latin *lugere*, to mourn; the same root as lugubrious).

handsel (HAND-sul)

n. a token of luck or good wishes given at the beginning of some enterprise. Also: money given as a token of good fortune in the new year.

> Gretel and Hansel
> could have used a handsel
> before their trip
> to avoid the witch's grip.

eleemosynary (el-uh-MAHSS-uh-ner-ee)

adj. pertaining to alms; supported by charity; charitable.

solmization (SAHL-mih-ZAY-shun)

n. the system of using a set of syllables to the tones of a musical scale.

> The von Trapps' education
> in solmization
> began with "Doe a deer,"
> which helps train the ear.

Lydian (LID-ee-un)

adj. pertaining to a mode of ancient Greek music that is characterized as soft, sweet and effeminate (originally called Ionian, after a tribe of Greeks who were despised as "soft" by their more militarily inclined counterparts, the Dorians; a naming error resulted in subsequent references to this musical mode as Lydian). *n.* in medieval and modern music, a major scale that raises the fourth note by a semi-tone.

froward (FRŌ-wurd)

adj. tending to disobey; contrary; uncooperative (from the Old English *fromweard*, opposite of toward).

> No word
> can force froward
> children to obey.
> They'll just say,
> "No way!"

unregenerate (un-rih-JEN-ur-it)

adj. unreformed; unconverted; obstinate.

> Ladies, don't try to reform unregenerate men or it
> will frustrate you,
> and they'll hate you.

engagé (EN-gah-ZHAY)

adj. actively committed, esp. to a political cause.

dégagé (DAY-gah-ZHAY)

adj. unconstrained by conventions; carefree.

> Someone dégagé is relaxed,
> while someone engagé acts.
> One prefers to sit it out;
> the other will protest and shout.

deictic (DĪK-tik)

adj. proving directly; not requiring the support of indirect arguments—e.g., the statement "It is raining outside now" can be proved simply by looking outside. Also: pertaining to a word whose specific meaning can be determined only by its context—e.g., "then," "there" or "you" (from the Greek *deiktikos*, able to show).

elenctic (ih-LENGK-tik)

adj. relating to a refuting argument, and often applied to indirect modes of proof (from the Greek *elenctikos*, fond of refuting).

> Says the baker: "Key lime is the best of pies."
> "Not if you trade cream of tartar for lye!"
> says his wife, whose elenctic refutation
> leads her husband to revise his observation:
> "Only a recipe followed as planned
> produces lime pie worth the moniker 'grand.'"

reductio ad absurdum
(rih-DUK-tee-ō ad ab-SUR-dum)

reductiones ad absurdum
(rih-duk-tee-Ō-neez ad ab-SUR-dum)

n., n.pl. the refutation of an argument or proposition by pushing it to an absurd logical extreme.

> Reductiones ad absurdum—
> everybody's heard 'em:
> If everything I say is untrue,
> then "I'm lying" would be untrue too!

dystopia (diss-TŌ-pee-uh)

n. an imaginary place or state in which living

conditions are as bad as possible, as from deprivation, oppression or terror.

> Orwell's alleged utopian state
> was really a dystopia—a trait
> that caused the *1984* hero to feel
> compunction
> about the state's dysfunction.

Jacobin (JAK-uh-bin)

n. a political radical; an extremist (after the Jacobins, a revolutionary group that implemented the French Revolution's Reign of Terror, so called because they first met at the Church of Saint Jacques convent).

> The Jacobins
> were supposed to be fairer,
> not attack and rob in
> a reign of terror.

donnish (DON-ish)

adj. stuffily academic; resembling a university professor, or don.

> Someone donnish
> can astonish
> with airs of academia.
> I prefer Bohemia.

luddite (LUD-īt)

n. an opponent of technological progress (after a group of early 19th-century British workers who destroyed weaving machinery in the belief that the new technology would cost them their jobs; named after Ned Ludd, an English laborer believed to have done the same).

miche (MICH)

v.i. to lurk or lie hidden; skulk; slink.

> I miche
> to avoid a snitch.
> I slink
> to avoid the clink.

fordo (fawr-DOO)

v.t. to do away with; kill. Also: to destroy; ruin; wreck.

> Fordo
> you?
> Never.
> You're far too clever.

pestiferous (peh-STIH-fur-uss)

adj. bringing or bearing disease; pestilential. Also: pernicious; morally evil.

syncretism (SIN-krih-tiz-um)

n. the attempted union of different or opposing beliefs or philosophies; reconciliation of opposing thought systems, sometimes for the purpose of resisting the influence of yet another system threatening to these.

verism (VIHR-iz-um)

n. realism or focus on the mundane, rather than the heroic or romantic, in art or literature.

> There's a clear schism
> between proponents of verism
> and romantics
> with their myths gigantic.

veriest (VEHR-ee-ist)

adj. truest; most genuine; most complete (superlative of very).

> As merry
> is to merriest,
> very
> is to veriest.

illusor (ih-LOO-sur)

n. one who deludes; a deceiver.

sclerous (SKLEER-uss)

adj. hard; bony; toughened.

> You may fear us
> because we're sclerous—
> as hard and bony
> as raw macaroni.

eburnean (ih-BUR-nee-un)

adj. ivory-like or made of ivory.

> Some folks Hibernian
> have skin eburnean—
> that is, complexions fairer
> than some south of Eire.

foramen (fuh-RAY-min)
foramina (fuh-RAY-mih-nuh)

n., n.pl. a small opening, perforation or orifice, esp. in an organ, husk, bone, etc.

ephectic (ih-FEK-tik)

adj. habitually putting off judgment; reflexively skeptical.

> If you don't tend to judge
> and are willing to budge,
> then you're ephectic—
> ideal for dialectic!

epoche (EP-uh-kee)

n. the suspension of judgment or belief.

putamen (pyoo-TAY-men)

n. a hard, shell-like covering, such as that enclosing the kernel of a peach. Also: the reddish outer layer of gray matter in the lentil-shaped nucleus of the brain.

> What the botanist calls a putamen
> is a peach pit to the layman.
> Whichever name fits,
> it's still the pits.

farrier (FA-ree-ur)

n. one who shoes horses; a blacksmith.

> A mare can keep pace
> during a chase
> with help from the farrier,
> who makes shoes to carry her.

ungulate (UNG-gyuh-lit)

adj. having hooves; resembling hooves.

gravid (GRAV-id)

adj. pregnant (from the Latin *gravidus*, heavy).

pavid (PAV-id)

adj. fearful; frightened; timid.

> Rosemary, gravid,
> became very pavid
> when she found out that maybe
> she bore Lucifer's baby.

sylvatic (sil-VAT-ik)

adj. affecting only wild animals. Also: pertaining to the woods; sylvan.

swain (SWĀN)

n. a male admirer; suitor. Also: one who lives and works in the country or on a farm.

> Lovers' Lane
> is home to the swain.
> It's where the lover
> can find cover.

Corydon (KAWR-ih-dun)

n. a generic proper name for a shepherd or swain in pastoral poetry, a genre of verse portraying rural life.

> Of Corydons
> there's more than one.
> Virgil's shepherd was among the first,
> and these rustics still populate
> pastoral verse.

rustication (RUSS-tih-KAY-shun)

n. country living. Also: in architecture, the beveling of the edges of stone blocks to emphasize the joints between them.

selcouth (SEL-kooth)

adj. strange; uncommon; arousing wonder.

> That which is selcouth
> in truth
> should not be feared
> just because it's weird.

dithyrambic (DIH-thih-RAM-bik)

adj. wildly enthusiastic. Also: like a dithyramb, a short lyric that's usually passionate or intensely emotional.

Verse that's dithyrambic
need not be trochaic or iambic,
but must be enthusiastic—
like this poem. Fantastic!

gratulate (GRACH-uh-lāt)

v.t. to express joy at; express happiness on behalf of.

sural (SUR-ul)

adj. pertaining to the calf of the leg.

The word sural
concerns the calf—
not the type you find in pastures rural,
but on a person's lower half.

funambulist (fyoo-NAM-byuh-list)

n. a tightrope walker.

The fun and fabulous
funambulist
crosses the tightrope
(we hope).

theandric (thee-AN-drik)

adj. partaking of both the human and the divine (ult. from the Greek *theandros*, god-man).

fatidic (fuh-TID-ik)

adj. pertaining to prophecy; prophetic (ult. from the Latin *fatum*, fate, and *dicere*, to say or utter).

> A critic
> of the fatidic
> says "Get off it!"
> to the prophet.

mantic (MAN-tik)

adj. pertaining to the power of divination; prophetic (from the Greek *mantikós*, of a soothsayer).

> A man who's mantic
> can predict
> the future—
> but how well, we're not too sure.

ka (KAH)

n. in ancient Egyptian religion, a spiritual part of a human being that survived after death and could reside in a statue of the deceased.

fugle (FYOO-guhl)

v.i. to signal; to gesture as if signaling. Also: to act as a guide, model or leader (from fugleman, a soldier serving as a model for his company during drills).

> The fugleman
> signals heavily
> while the bugleman
> plays morning reveille.

brassard (bruh-SAHRD)

n. a cloth band or badge worn on the upper arm (often braided or tasseled).

> A member of the Royal Guard
> proudly wears his brassard—
> a braided badge on his upper arm
> marking him and his fellows as
> protectors from harm.

bayadère (BĪ-uh-DEHR)

n. a fabric of contrasting horizontal stripes, often in brilliant colors (originally, the French word for a female dancer from India who wore this fabric; ult. from the Latin *ballare*, to dance, the same root as ballet). *adj.* striped.

> Bayadère
> is dancewear
> with stripes
> of the horizontal type.

cheviot (SHEV-ee-ut)

n. a woolen fabric in a coarse twill weave, from a breed of sheep noted for its short, thick wool (originally from the Cheviot Hills in England and Scotland).

pleonasm (PLEE-uh-naz-um)

n. the use of more words than are necessary to express an idea.

> Ah, the pleonasm:
> Almost all circulars have 'em.
> "Free gift" or "winning prize"
> are their redundantly phrased cries.

mountebank (MOUN-tih-bangk)

n. a flamboyant charlatan; a fraud (literally, "one who climbs up on a bench" in Italian; the word originally referred to an itinerant who would hawk quack medicine from a raised platform, often using various entertainments to attract a crowd).

> We have the Internet to thank
> for the ascendance of the mountebank,
> who hawks sundry remedies
> to treat male extremities.

saltimbanco (sawl-tim-BON-kō)

n. a mountebank; a quack (literally, "one who leaps up on a bench" in Italian).

chine (CHĪN)

n. the backbone or spine of an animal; a cut of meat including this. Also: a ridge or crest.

> A chine
> is a spine.
> Not every creature
> has this feature.

grume (GROOM)

n. a thick, viscous fluid, esp. a clot of blood.

claggy (KLAG-ee)

adj. tending to form sticky lumps or clots; sticky; gummy. Also: muddy.

> Anyone got a Baggie?
> This taffy is claggy—
> so sticky,
> it's icky.

stramineous (struh-MIN-ee-uss)

adj. consisting of straw; straw-like.

> It's not ignominious
> to be stramineous.
> Ask the scarecrow—
> he'll know.

dissilient (dih-SIL-ee-unt)

adj. bursting apart, like some seed pods when ripe.

eruct (ih-RUKT)

v.t., v.i. to belch forth, as gas from the stomach; issue violently, like lava from a volcano.

> At the table he eructed
> with a belch unobstructed.
> When his tummy erupts,
> it can be quite abrupt.

picaresque (pik-uh-RESK)

adj. pertaining to stories about clever, adventurous rogues, usually of low social status.

> Henry Fielding, at his desk,
> wrote novels most picaresque,
> involving heroes charming
> who were knavish yet disarming.

farrow (FA-rō)

adj. not producing calves in a season (esp. of cows).

farrow (FA-rō)

n. a litter of pigs. *v.t., v.i.* to produce a litter, esp. of pigs.

> A cow that's farrow
> is lying fallow,
> while a sow that farrows a litter
> needs a critter-sitter.

genesic (juh-NESS-ik)

adj. pertaining to genesis or reproduction.

agenesic (ay-jin-ESS-ik)

adj. characterized by sterility; infertile.

> Some agenesic
> wish they could lick

the hurdle
of being infertile.

gynecic (jih-NEE-sik)

adj. pertaining to women.

> Guys who fear gals
> have absurd rationales,
> such as "Matters gynecic
> tend to make me sick."

philogynous (fih-LAH-jih-nuss)

adj. loving women; fond of women.

> Though a man philogynous
> is superior to a man misogynous,
> a man's love of women
> can also do him in.

oniomania (ō-nee-uh-MAY-nee-uh)

n. an uncontrollable urge to buy things.

> Oh no! My mania
> is oniomania.
> You can't stop me from buying,
> but thank you for trying.

trichotillomania (TRIK-uh-til-uh-MAY-nee-uh)

n. chronic hair-pulling.

fillip (FIL-lip)

n. a sharp, striking blow made by a snapping of the finger against the thumb. Also: a trifle. *v.i.* to gesture with a fillip.

> A fillip
> is a finger flip,
> like a snap
> or a smart tap.

onychophagy (ON-ih-KAH-fuh-jee)

n. chronic nail-biting.

> I suffer onychophagy
> and bite my nails off, you see,
> whether I'm distressed
> or feeling depressed.

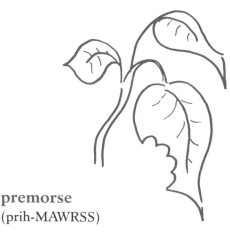

premorse
(prih-MAWRSS)

adj. appearing bitten off (usually used to apply to a leaf or root).

> Good grief!
> Who took a bite of this leaf?
> Now that the foliage is premorse,
> I hope the biter feels remorse.

repand (rih-PAND)

adj. having a somewhat wavy edge (usually of a leaf).

> Something repand
> does not wave, like a hand—
> but is what one sees
> on the edge of some leaves.

liturate (LICH-ur-āt)

adj. having indistinct spots.

maculate (MAK-yuh-lut)

adj. spotted or blemished; besmirched; impure.

maculate (MAK-yuh-lāt)

v.t. to pollute; sully.

> A surface maculate
> has spots,
> while one immaculate
> does not.

cuneate (KYOO-nee-āt)

adj. wedge-shaped.

> I know not how one so puny ate
> that huge cuneate
> piece of cake—
> for goodness' sake!

sulcate (SUHL-kāt)

adj. having deep grooves or furrows.

touchstone (TUCH-stōn)

n. a test or criterion for determining the quality of a thing (literally, a stone that tests the quality of gold).

> There's no better stone
> than the touchstone
> for gauging the quality of the gold
> that you hold.

rupicolous (roo-PIK-uh-luhs)

adj. living in or growing among rocks.

> You think I'm rupicolous?
> I'm in shock.
> That's ridiculous!
> I don't live under a rock.

vug (VUG)

n. a small cavity in a rock or mineral vein.

sumptuary (SUMP-choo-ehr-ee)

adj.   regulating   or   controlling   expenses,

commercial matters or real estate activities. Also: regulating, on moral or religious grounds, personal behavior.

> To ban a mansion rambling
> or forbid a house of gambling—
> both are considered very
> plainly sumptuary.

cabotage (KAB-uh-tazh)

n. the right of a country to restrict air traffic within its borders.

> To minimize sabotage
> a nation will use cabotage
> to restrict traffic by air
> and prevent a scare.

vendition (ven-DISH-un)

n. the act of vending; the act of selling goods for a living.

leeftail (LEEF-tāl)

adj. in great demand; quick-selling.

bowdlerize (BŌD-lur-īz)

v.t. to prudishly abridge; expurgate in a manner that distorts meaning (after Thomas Bowdler's expurgated "family" edition of Shakespeare in 1818; for example, in *Henry IV, Part 2*, the character Doll Tearsheet, a prostitute, is omitted entirely).

> They bowdlerize
> to shield your eyes
> from text
> that's oversexed.

coprolite (KOP-ruh-LĪT)

n. fossilized excrement; petrified dung.

To be polite,
in a fight,
use *coprolite*
when you don't see fit
to use a word like it.

reliquiae (rih-LIK-wee-ee)

n.pl. mortal remains, esp. of animals or plants; fossils.

One day we'll be
reliquiae—
no more than docile
old fossils.

edaphic (ih-DAF-ik)

adj. pertaining to the soil; influenced by soil conditions rather than climate.

pratal (PRAY-dul)

adj. pertaining to meadows; living in meadows (from the Latin *pratum*, a meadow, the same root as prairie).

Since the cradle
I've dreamed of the pratal—
of meadows
where grass grows.

bosky (BAHSS-kee)

adj. woody; covered with bushes, shrubs or small trees.

This area's so bosky,
I'll never find my lost key.
The place is so wooded,
I'll never find where I put it.

scandent (SKAN-dunt)

adj. climbing, esp. of a plant.

preagonal (pree-AG-uh-nuhl)

adj. immediately preceding death (literally, before agony).

> The moment preagonal
> I imagine'll
> be the last tranquil breath
> before the onset of death.

saprogenic (SAP-rō-JEN-ik)

adj. causing or pertaining to decay or putrefaction.

> Bacteria saprogenic
> are highly unhygienic;
> their mission
> is decomposition.

cicatrize (SIK-uh-TRĪZ)

v.t., *v.i.* to heal by scar tissue formation.

privity (PRIV-ih-tee)

n. knowledge of a private matter, esp. when the knowledge implies approval or consent. Also: in law, the relationship between multiple parties resulting from their mutual participation or interest in a transaction.

countermand (koun-tur-MAND)

v.t. to issue a command or order reversing an earlier one; revoke. *n.* an order or command reversing an earlier one.

> To countermand
> is to counter a command.
> That order I signed?
> Now I say, "Never mind."

oeillade (oo-YOD)

n. an amorous glance; ogling.

> Trade a blatant oeillade
> for a genteel facade.
> A lusty glance
> won't lead to romance.

nates (NAY-teez)

n.pl. buttocks; rump.

> If I threaten to kick your nates
> to Hades,
> I'm threatening to kick your butt
> to you know what!

buccal (BUK-uhl)

adj. pertaining to the cheek.

> A punch to the region buccal
> with your knuckle
> is a blow to the cheek,
> so to speak.

barbate (BAHR-bāt)

adj. bearded.

lycanthrope (LĪ-kun-thrōp)

n. a person with the delusion of being a wolf.

> The lycanthrope
> can hope
> his howls at the moon
> are in tune.

imbricate (IM-brih-kit)

adj. overlapping or layered, as scales or roofing tiles.

imbricate (IM-brih-kāt)

v.t., v.i. to overlap in a pattern like that of tiles.

decussate (DIH-kuss-ĀT)

v.t., v.i. to cross or become crossed; intersect so as to form an X.

> When two lines decussate,
> an X-shape they create.
> In olden days, X's were
> what some used as their signature.

omphalos (OM-fuh-luss)
omphali (OM-fuh-lī)

n., n.pl. a central point; hub. Literally: the navel.

> Los Angeles
> is the omphalos
> of the movie biz—
> where the action is.

theodolite (thee-OD-uh-līt)

n. an instrument used by surveyors for measuring angles by means of a small, mounted, rotating telescope.

chresmologue (KRESS-muh-log)

n. a compiler of oracles.

> A chresmologue's
> job is to log
> oracles
> in an order categorical.

afflatus (uh-FLAY-tuss)

n. a creative impulse, imparting of knowledge or inspiration of divine origin.

> With your muse on hiatus,
> you lose your afflatus.
> Without her spark,
> you're in the dark.

chiliad (KIL-ee-ad)

n. a period of 1,000 years. Also: a group of 1,000.

> There was a chiliad
> between events in the *Iliad*

and the creation of the Rosetta stone:
a thousand years, as far as is known.

draconic (druh-KON-ik)

adj. pertaining to a dragon; dragon-like.

> A creature draconic
> causes shifts tectonic
> with each mighty puff
> of that fiery stuff.

prochronism (PRŌ-kruh-niz-um)

n. an error in chronology that places something or someone in a time period earlier than the actual one.

parachronism (puh-RAK-ruh-niz-um)

n. an error in chronology that places something or someone in a time period later than the actual one.

> A prochronism is a motor car
> appearing in the 2nd century B.C.E.
> A parachronism equally bizarre
> is a Neanderthal selling car insurance on TV.

aoristic (ay-uh-RISS-tik)

adj. not occurring in a specified time period; indefinite; indeterminate.

> It helps to determine the time
> when solving a crime.
> Events aoristic
> don't create a reference point realistic.

coffle (KAW-fuhl)

n. a chained line of slaves, prisoners or animals.

> A coffle
> is an awful
> line of chained labor.
> Do it not unto thy neighbor!

oubliette (OO-blee-ET)

n. a jail cell with a trap door in the ceiling as the only opening (from the French *oublier*, to forget, as jailers often left prisoners in such a room to forget about them).

> They'll forget
> they threw you in an oubliette.
> Once through the trap door,
> you'll be heard from no more.

prescind (prih-SIND)

v.t. to cut off abruptly. *v.i.* to withdraw attention.

agnomination (ag-NOM-ih-NAY-shun)

n. the use of two similar-sounding words, or the repetition of one word in two different senses, for humorous effect. Also: punning.

> Agnomination
> gets my nomination
> for "most likely to evince a groan."
> Punning's a habit I've not outgrown.

parisology (pa-riss-OL-uh-jee)

n. the use of ambiguous language; equivocation (from the Greek *parisos*, almost equal, evenly balanced).

> My parisology
> requires an apology.
> I meant Paris the town,
> not the one in the gown.

auscultation (AW-skul-TAY-shun)

n. the act of listening, esp. in diagnosis, to sounds within organs such as the heart or lungs, as an aid in diagnosis, directly or with a stethoscope.

> Careful auscultation
> can detect a palpitation.
> By listening,
> docs don't miss a thing.

somatic (sō-MAT-ik)

adj. pertaining to the body; physical.

> He was emphatic
> that his condition was somatic.
> We were gentle
> when we told him it was mental.

gnathal (NAY-thuhl)

adj. pertaining to the jaw.

chassé (sha-SAY)

v.i. to execute a series of gliding dance steps in which one foot takes the place of the other. *n.* such a series of steps (from the French; literally, "chased").

> The French chassé
> at fancy balls.
> Americans sashay
> in overalls.

pronate (PRŌ-nāt)

v.t., v.i. to rotate the hand so the palm faces down or back. Also: to stand with the weight on the inner edge of the feet (from the Latin *pronatus*, bent forward).

> To pronate
> means to rotate
> your hand so the palm faces down,
> or your foot so the inner edge is on
> the ground.

discalced (diss-KALST)

adj. unshod or wearing sandals (used esp. of members of strict religious orders, such as the Discalced Carmelites, an order founded by St. Teresa of Avila and St. John of the Cross in the late 1500s).

apostasy (uh-PAHSS-tuh-see)

n. renunciation of one's religion, political affiliation, etc.

peccant (PEH-kuhnt)

adj. sinning; offending; in violation of a rule; at fault.

> On the day things are reckoned,
> those who were peccant
> will surely get theirs—
> so mind your affairs.

yisser (YISS-ur)

n. a covetous person.

> Some say a yisser
> deserves one in the kisser.
> Sure, it's wrong to covet,
> but who's above it?

ai (Ī)

n. a type of sloth native to South America.

jejune (jih-JOON)

adj. without substance. Also: immature; juvenile.

> Poems rhyming "June" and "moon"
> are to me so jejune.
> Still, I wouldn't diss one,
> not even this one.

quidnunc (KWID-nungk)

n. a gossip; busybody; an overly inquisitive or nosy person (from the Latin *quid nunc?* or "what now?").

> Who's a cheat and who's a drunk?
> Ask the office quidnunc.
> On such gossip he's keen,
> betraying any secret he can glean.

haver (HAY-vur)

v.i. to talk garrulously and foolishly; chatter. Also: to hesitate; put off deciding.

mesic (MEZ-ik)

adj. characterized by or adapted to an environment having a moderate supply of moisture.

> It's hard to get sick
> in an atmosphere mesic.
> Therefore, rejoice, for
> you have sufficient moisture.

pobby (PAH-bee)

adj. soft; pulpy; bloated; swollen (from "pobs," pieces of bread softened in milk).

tyrosis (tī-RŌ-siss)

n. curdling of milk, esp. in the stomach.

viviparous (vī-VIP-ur-uss)

adj. producing living young, as most mammals do, instead of eggs.

> So hip for us
> to be viviparous.
> It's out of date
> to lay eggs and wait.

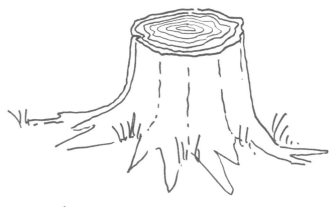

annulose (AN-yuh-LŌSS)

adj. ringed or ringlike; made up of rings or ringlike parts.

> Trees are annulose—
> a ring per year they boast
> after you core them,
> to see when a seed bore them.

dendritic (den-DRIH-tik)

adj. branching like a tree.

viaticum (vī-AT-ih-kum)

n. a travel allowance or travel supplies.

> My viaticum
> is a hat 'n some
> sandals and money,
> when headed someplace sunny.

farrago (fuh-RAH-gō)

n. a hodgepodge; confused medley.

> Her writings are a farrago
> of thoughts about Chicago,
> Dr. Zhivago
> and stories of Santiago.

comfit (KUM-fit)

n. a candy consisting of a sugared nut or piece of fruit; a confection.

discomfit (diss-KUM-fit)

v.t. to undo in battle; defeat or overthrow completely; rout. Also: to confuse; disconcert.

> Although I'm on a diet,
> the cravings I cannot quiet.
> This comfit that I'm chewing
> discomfits all I'm doing.

enallage (en-AL-uh-jee)

n. the switching from one grammatical form to another (e.g., from third to first person), or the replacement of a correct grammatical form with an incorrect form for rhetorical effect.

> "We was robbed!"
> the coach sobbed.
> Bad grammar? Sure it be—
> a perfect example of enallage.

postpositive (pōst-POZ-ih-tiv)

adj. coming after, rather than before, a word to modify it or to show its relation to other elements of a sentence.

> To end a line with an adjective
> in poetry, make it postpositive.
> Put the word after the noun—
> for example, "the bag brown."

obelus (OB-ih-luss)

n. a symbol (— or ÷) used in ancient manuscripts to mark the beginning of a doubtful or spurious passage.

pensée (pon-SAY)

n. a thought or reflection, esp. expressed in literary form.

> Pensée
> is a word *français*.
> It means a thought—
> for pennies, Pascal's can be bought.

opsimath (OP-sih-math)

n. a person who becomes a student later in life.

> An opsimath
> takes the path
> of learning late.
> It's worth the wait!

climacteric (klī-MAK-tur-ik)

n. a critical stage, esp. a period of a person's life, marked by important physiological or psychic change, such as menopause for women. *adj.* pertaining to such a stage.

nonce (NONSS)

n. the present occasion; particular instance.

> For the nonce
> I'm ensconced
> in my *chaise longue*—
> is that so wrong?

salvific (sal-VIH-fik)

adj. pertaining to redemptive power; having the power of salvation.

> Images beatific
> have a power salvific,
> sometimes even saving
> people from their raving.

precant (PREK-unt)

n. a person who prays.

> To preserve his soul,
> the atheist in the foxhole
> will become a precant
> within a second.

laicity (lay-IH-sih-tee)

n. the principles, rules or influence of lay people as opposed to clergy.

parrhesia (puh-REEZ-yuh)

n. boldness in speaking; frankness. Also: the act of asking forgiveness in advance for speaking with candor.

> If my speech doesn't please ya,
> I must plead parrhesia.
> So don't meet my boldness
> with coldness.

raillery (RĀL-ur-ee)

n. good-natured teasing; banter.

persiflage (PUR-sih-flozh)

n. light, good-natured discussion; banter.

> Persiflage
> can camouflage
> sharp barbs expressed
> in gentle jest.

barton (BART-un)

n. a poultry yard or chicken coop. Also: a large farm or manor.

> I pick fruits from my garden
> and eggs from my barton,
> home of my chicken coop
> and the rest of my poultry troupe.

olitory (OL-ih-TAWR-ee)

adj. pertaining to a kitchen garden; produced in a kitchen garden.

> Now I'm taking inventory
> of my herbs olitory.
> Then I'll start in
> picking more from my garden.

tuckahoe (TUK-uh-hō)

n. various plants or plant parts used by some Native Americans as food, such as the roots of the golden-club and certain fungi.

obtest (ob-TEST)

v.t. to invoke as a witness. Also: to beseech; entreat.

> I tried to obtest
> the lady distressed,
> but the court questioned her fitness
> as a witness.

suborn (suh-BAWRN)

v.t. to cause to commit perjury; bribe or induce to commit a misdeed or crime.

> I scorn
> one who tries to suborn
> me to commit a misdeed
> by appealing to greed.

intercalate (in-TUR-kuh-lāt)

v.t. to insert into, esp. to add extra days in a calendar.

To intercalate
means to insert dates
in a calendar, to match the seasons
for solar and lunar reasons.

recondite (REK-un-dīt)

adj. profound; beyond common knowledge.

If you say something recondite,
I, for a second, might
try to pretend
that I comprehend.

abstruse (ab-STROOSS)

adj. difficult to understand; esoteric.

Ideas abstruse
are not in heavy use.
They're in low demand
since they're hard to understand.

ravelment (RAV-ul-munt)

n. confusion; entanglement.

limacine (LIM-uh-sīn)

adj. sluglike or pertaining to slugs.

Only the dim assign
the limacine
to run a race.
A slug can't keep pace.

oscine (AH-sīn)

adj. pertaining to songbirds.

Ah, sing sublime,
you bird oscine!
I've heard
you're a good songbird.

jabiru (JAB-ih-roo)

n. a large tropical American stork having white plumage, a pink band at the neck and a naked head.

accipitrine (ak-SIP-ih-TRĪN)

adj. predatorial; hawklike. Literally: belonging to the avian genus *Accipiter*, which includes hawks.

> Pity the pigeon in the pine
> eyed by the hawk accipitrine,
> who's predatorially inclined
> and in the mood to dine.

chevy (CHEV-ee)

v.t. to chase or harass. *n.* a chase or hunt.

> Chevy means chase.
> Thus "Chevy Chase"
> is a redundancy,
> as anyone can see.

parkour (pahr-KOOR)

n. a system of leaps, vaults, rolls and landings intended to help a person avoid or surmount whatever lies in his or her path; the art of efficient flight or pursuit (a neologism derived from the French *parcours*, route; the discipline was invented in France in the 1990s and was featured in the opening scene of the 2007 James Bond film *Casino Royale*).

traceur (TRAY-sur)
traceuse (TRAY-sooss)

n. a person who practices parkour (traceur is the masculine; traceuse, the feminine).

> The traceur and traceuse
> need a masseur or masseuse
> after leaping and vaulting
> without halting.

limpet (LIM-pit)

n. one who clings persistently, esp. an official in a useless position who clings to his or her office. Literally: a mollusk found clinging to rocks on beaches.

> A limpet
> is a sea pet
> stuck to a rock,
> or a useless bureaucrat
> whose job we mock.

desipience (dih-SIP-ee-unss)

n. silliness; foolishness; extreme triviality.

lepid (LEP-id)

adj. pleasant; evoking amusement; witty.

> Something lepid
> evokes reactions far from tepid,
> whether a comedic ditty
> or a remark that's witty.

impresa (im-PRAY-zuh)

n. an emblem, often with an accompanying motto.

> A good impresa
> can amaze ya.
> Here's one to try:
> New Hampshire's "Live free or die."

sweal (SWEEL)

v.t. to singe; burn by scorching.

> I will squeal, see,
> if you sweal me.
> I come unhinged
> when I'm singed.

intactible (in-TAK-tih-buhl)

adj. imperceptible to the touch.

comminate (KOM-ih-nāt)

v.t., *v.i.* to threaten with divine vengeance; denounce formally; curse.

> To comminate
> is to threaten that fate
> will your body smite
> if you don't do right.

sectary (SEK-tuh-ree)

n. a member of a sect, particularly one regarded as heretical or schismatic; one who is zealously devoted to a sect.

ensorcell (en-SAWR-sul)

v.t. to enchant; bewitch.

> The magician Merlin employed spells
> on Arthur's enemies, to ensorcell
> any who threatened the King's Round Table,
> 'til adultery tragically ended the fable.

sortilege (SAWR-tul-ij)

n. sorcery; magic. Also: divination by drawing lots.

> Using sortilege,
> I can conjure a fort or bridge
> with a magic spell,
> and I've got one to sell.

nocent (NŌ-sint)

adj. not innocent; doing harm or having a tendency to harm; hurtful.

recrudescent (REE-kroo-DESS-int)

adj. breaking out again, as a disease or epidemic; renewed; renewing.

> The convalescent
> fears illness recrudescent.
> The patient spurns
> a disease's return.

diathesis (dī-ATH-ih-siss)

n. an inherited predisposition to certain illnesses or conditions. Also: a constitutional predisposition to certain evils.

compendious (kum-PEN-dee-uss)

adj. concise; succinct; comprehensively summarized.

bathetic (ba-THEH-tik)

adj. characterized by excessive pathos; overly sentimental; trite.

> My life's so bathetic,
> it's pathetic.
> So boring,
> you'll be snoring.

contemn (kun-TEM)

v.t. to regard or treat with disdain, scorn or contempt.

> Why such contempt
> for folks unkempt?
> Why the need to contemn
> all of them?

senary (SEN-uh-ree)

adj. pertaining to the number 6; having six items or parts.

> A hundred is centenary.
> Six is plenty senary—
> a cousin
> to "half a dozen."

coriaceous (kawr-ee-AY-shuss)

adj. leather-like; leathery. Also: stiff; tough.

limpid (LIM-pid)

adj. transparently clear; pellucid. Also: easily

intelligible; clearly expressed.

> You don't have to skimp, kid,
> to write in a style that's limpid.
> Just write clearly—
> your readers will thank you dearly.

scumble (SKUM-buhl)

v.t. to blur the outlines of; soften the colors of. Literally: to soften the colors or outlines of a painting or drawing by applying a thin coat of opaque or semiopaque color or by rubbing with a finger.

stipple (STIP-uhl)

v.t. to paint, draw or mark by means of dots or short strokes. *n.* the effect produced by stippling.

> With a stipple
> you can produce a ripple
> by means of lots
> of little dots.

cloche (KLŌSH)

n. a bell-shaped hat. Also: a bell-shaped cover for a plant or food.

> To some, the cloche
> is gauche.
> To others, the bell-shaped hat
> is where it's at.

Rare WORDS II

cache-peigne (KASH-pān)

n. ornamental trimming, usually worn at the back of a woman's hat (from the French *cacher*, to hide, and *peigne*, comb).

gravic (GRAV-ik)

adj. pertaining to gravitation; exerting gravitational force.

agravic (ay-GRAV-ik)

adj. pertaining to a state of zero gravity.

> A state agravic
> causes havoc.
> Put a lid on your cup,
> because liquid falls up!

samizdat (SAH-miz-dot)

n. an underground press; the illegal, secret publication and distribution of literature, esp. in the former Soviet Union. Also: the literature produced by this system.

> I confess—
> I was running a press
> until the commisar stopped
> my samizdat.

puissant (PWISS-unt)

adj. powerful; potent.

> A leader puissant
> is sometimes resistant
> to apportioning his power
> and is not known to cower.

surd (SURD)

n. a number that cannot be expressed as a ratio of whole numbers, as *pi;* an irrational number. Also: a speech sound that is not voiced. *adj.* lacking reason or sense; irrational (from the

Latin *surdus*, deaf or insufferable to the ear; the same root as absurd).

chevelure (shev-uh-LOOR)

n. a head of hair.

> Sorry to dishevel your
> chevelure.
> I know you put such care
> into your hair.

mullet (MUHL-it)

n. a hairstyle that is short in the front and on the sides and long in the back.

occiput (OK-sih-puht)

n. the back part of the head or skull.

> My locks stay put
> on my occiput.
> Don't pull it—
> you'll muss the mullet.

encephalon (en-SEF-uh-lon)

n. the brain of a vertebrate.

> Don't fall on
> your encephalon.
> It's a pain
> in the brain.

propitiate (prō-PISH-ee-ĀT)

v.t. to appease; conciliate.

> In World War II, the Vichy state
> was prone to propitiate—
> that is, to appease
> the invading Nazis.

neoteric (nee-uh-TEHR-ik)

adj. modern in origin; recent.

> An idea neoteric
> can prove esoteric—
> modern and new
> but understood by few.

quondam (KWON-dum)

adj. former; onetime.

> He was a chum
> 'til he conned 'em.
> Now the scum
> is a pal quondam.

rapporteur (RAP-awr-TUR)

n. someone who gives reports at meetings; an official charged with reporting findings of a commission back to some deliberative body.

> A rapporteur,
> whether him or her,
> is a meeting recorder—
> rather like a reporter.

misprision (miss-PRIZH-un)

n. neglect or violation of official duty; misconduct. Also: failure to prevent or report a serious crime.

analeptic (an-uh-LEP-tik)

n. an invigorating medication; a stimulant. *adj.* stimulating; restorative.

> To a skeptic,
> an analeptic
> can restore
> no more
> than a placebo.
> What does he know?

asthenic (ass-THEH-nik)

n. a physically weak or slender person. *adj.* physically weak. Also: having a slender physique.

> Some into eugenics
> might breed only asthenics,
> but a range of physiques
> is less dull than all sleek.

enteron (EN-tuh-RON)
entera (EN-ter-UH)

n., *n.pl.* the digestive tract; the intestines.

distrait (diss-TRAY)

adj. inattentive because of anxiety; distracted.

> I'm distrait
> from stray thoughts,
> far away
> because I'm distraught.

scrutoire (skroo-TWAHR)

n. a writing desk; escritoire.

> Whether I'm scribbling at my scrutoire
> or brooding in my boudoir,
> my thoughts coalesce
> around you, I confess.

monopsony (mun-OP-suh-nee)

n. a market condition in which there is only one buyer and many sellers (as opposed to monopoly, in which there is only one seller).

algesia (al-JEE-zee-uh)

n. hypersensitivity to pain.

> If you suffer from algesia
> and you're stung by bees, ya
> might howl
> and utter oaths most foul.

sanative (SAN-uh-tiv)

adj. having the power to cure; healing; restorative (ult. from the Latin *sanare*, to cure; the same root as sanatorium).

misprize (miss-PRĪZ)

v.t. to despise or undervalue.

> Miss out on a prize
> and you feel misprized.
> You can't hide it—
> you feel slighted.

guerdon (GUR-dun)

v.t. to reward. *n.* a reward; something earned or gained; compensation.

> She placed third and
> was guerdoned
> with a bronze medal
> that proved her mettle.

premiate (PREE-mee-āt)

v.t. to award a prize.

docent (DŌ-sunt)

n. a guide in a museum or art gallery, usually a volunteer. Also: a university lecturer.

> A museum's docent
> usually gets no cent
> for leading a tour
> about an artist obscure.

cicerone (SISS-uh-RŌ-nee)

n. a person who guides sightseers.

> From Queens to Coney,
> the cicerone
> will ensure
> that you get a great tour.

gadroon (guh-DROON)

n. an elaborately carved or indented convex molding. Also: an ornamental band decorated with a continuous pattern, as on a silversmith's work.

aa (AH-ah)

n. lava having a rough surface; one of the two chief forms of lava emitted from volcanoes of the Hawaiian type (from the Hawaiian; it also means "to burn").

⚡ gramineous (gruh-MIN-ee-uss)

adj. pertaining to grass; grassy; belonging to the Gramineae family of plants (from the Latin *gramen*, grass).

blithen (BLĪ-*th*un)

v.t. to make blithe or carefree; cheer up; gladden.

> Cute kittens
> playing with mittens
> blithen me when I'm blue.
> Why, then, not you too?

maunder (MAWN-dur)

v.i. to talk or move aimlessly.

> To maunder
> is to wander
> aimlessly, as when you amble.
> It also means to ramble.

kinesics (kih-NEE-siks)

n. the study of body language and facial gestures as a means of communication.

> Kinesics
> studies those tics
> of body and face
> that words can't replace.

hydrargyrum (hī-DRAHR-jih-rum)

n. mercury; quicksilver (ult. from the Greek *hydrargyros*, liquid silver; the word is the source of the chemical symbol Hg).

gambol (GAM-buhl)

v.i. to skip about in play; frolic.

> Don't gambol
> in the bramble.
> It's more than tickly;
> it's downright prickly.

sessile (SESS-uhl)

adj. permanently attached and not freely moving. Also: sedentary.

> An object sessile,
> like a coral reef,
> could block a marine vessel
> and cause the captain grief.

lollop (LOL-up)

v.i. to lounge about. Also: to move with a bobbing motion.

> To lollop is to lounge around.
> It can also mean to bobble up and down.

testudinal (tess-TOO-dih-nol)

adj. pertaining to or resembling a tortoise or a tortoise shell.

scapular (SKAP-yuh-lur)

adj. pertaining to the shoulder or shoulder blade.
n. a monastic garment that covers the shoulders.

> If I tap you, good Sir,
> on the bone scapular,
> give me a scold,
> but not a shoulder that's cold.

febricity (fih-BRISS-ih-tee)

n. the state of having a fever; feverishness.

gyre (JĪ-ur)

n. a circular or spiral motion; a vortex.

> Tires
> makes gyres
> on the road;
> if not, the car's towed.

trochal (TRŌ-kuhl)

adj. wheel-shaped or wheel-like.

antiphon (AN-tih-fon)

n. a verse or psalm to be chanted or sung as a response.

> The antiphon
> is a verse or song
> where I call and you respond.

melisma (muh-LIZ-muh)

n. a group of several notes sung to one syllable of text, as in Middle Eastern music, blues and Gregorian chant.

> A melisma
> is one syllable sung with charisma.
> Pop stars far and wide
> on this technique have relied.

cavatina (kav-uh-TEE-nuh)

n. in opera, a simple melody or song, shorter than an aria.

> When I say cavatina,
> I mean a
> simple song
> that's not too long.

benison (BEH-ni-zen)

n. a blessing; benediction; something bestowed or appearing as a gift of grace or blessing.

doyen (doy-EN)

doyenne (doy-EN)

n. the senior or most prominent member of a group (doyen is the masculine; doyenne, the feminine).

> Don't annoy a hen
> who's the doyenne.
> She's sorta
> the top of the pecking order.

ophelimity (AH-ful-IH-mih-tee)

n. the capacity to satisfy a desire, want or need, usually in an economic sense (from the Greek *ophelimos*, useful or helpful).

chrematistics (kreh-muh-TISS-tiks)

n. the study of wealth.

> How did Croesus make his money?
> That's what chrematistics studies:
> whether he gained his wealth
> by luck or by stealth.

prebend (PREB-und)

n. a monetary allowance from the revenues of a church, granted to a clergyman as his stipend.

phratry (FRAY-tree)

n. a subdivision of a tribe; among the ancient Greeks, a kinship group made up of clans.

> Don't hate me
> because I'm in a different phratry.
> We should jibe,
> since we're in the same tribe.

sodality (sō-DA-lih-tee)

n. fellowship; comradeship.

> Sodality
> breeds congeniality.
> It's a big sip
> of comradeship.

helpmeet (HELP-meet)

n. one serving as a helper or companion, esp. a wife or husband.

apologue (AP-uh-log)

n. a moral fable. Also: an allegory.

> In Aesop's apologue
> about the wolf and the house dog,
> the wolf would rather live free
> than wear a collar and captive be.

cacodoxy (KAK-uh-DOKS-ee)

n. a wrong opinion or doctrine; perverse teachings; heresy.

scrutator (SKROO-tay-tur)

n. an investigator or examiner; one who scrutinizes.

> You don't need thumb screws
> to be a scrutator.
> There are other methods to use
> to be a good investigator.

dragoon (druh-GOON)

v.t. to try to compel into submission by using harsh or violent means.

> I was dragooned
> by a goon—
> trapped
> and kidnapped.

subluxate (sub-LUX-āt)

v.t. to dislocate partially or slightly.

mattock (MAT-uk)

n. a tool for digging in and loosening soil, resembling a pickax, with one end broad instead of pointed.

> A mattock
> makes soil less static.
> It's a big
> help on a dig.

chaff (CHAFF)

n. the parts of grains or grasses that are separated from the seed during threshing.

chaff (CHAFF)

v.t. to tease good-naturedly; banter. *n.* good-natured teasing; raillery.

facetiae (fuh-SEE-shee-ee)

n.pl. witty or humorous remarks and writings.

> To chaff
> a friend is to mock her for a laugh.
> Just go easy
> with the facetiae.

ensiform (EN-sih-fawrm)

adj. sword-shaped; having sharp edges and tapering to a thin point.

> Hold an object ensiform
> with a perfect fencing form.
> People will think it's a sword,
> and you won't be ignored.

acuminate (uh-KYOO-mih-nit)

adj. pointed; tapering to a point.

acuminate (uh-KYOO-mih-nāt)

v.t. to sharpen; to taper to a point (from the Latin *acuminare*, to point).

matutinal (muh-TOO-tin-uhl)

adj. pertaining to or occurring in the morning; early in the day.

> At her meal matutinal
> she eats her fruit 'n all
> of her corn flakes
> as soon as she wakes.

tiffin (TIF-in)

n. a midday meal; a light lunch.

> For tiffin
> I'll be sniffin'
> around noon.
> Feed me soon!

cenatory (SEN-uh-tawr-ree)

adj. pertaining to dinner; appropriate for dining.

> I eat chicken cacciatore
> at my meal cenatory.
> It's always a winner
> at dinner.

viands (VĪ-unds)

n.pl. provisions; articles of food.

depute (dih-PYOOT)

v.t. to appoint as deputy or agent.

> Sheriffs depute
> those of good repute,
> not vandals
> mired in scandals.

vernissage (VEHR-nih-SAZH)

n. a private art showing preceding an exhibition (literally, a varnishing; historically, the day before an art opening was reserved for an artist to varnish the paintings).

> I brought my entourage
> to the vernissage
> before the exhibition,
> with free admission.

impasto (im-PASS-tō)

n. the laying on of paint so thickly that the brush marks are visible. Also: paint laid on in this manner.

> I'd try impasto.
> The canvas is vast, though.
> I must use restraint
> so I don't run out of paint.

scagliola (skal-YŌ-la)

n. plasterwork imitating marble or stone.

sematic (sih-MAT-ik)

adj. serving to warn of danger.

> Like a park ranger
> warning of danger,
> a sign sematic
> can be quite dramatic.

montigenous (mon-TIJ-ih-nus)

adj. produced by mountains; native to mountain areas.

factitious (fak-TISH-us)

adj. artificial; manufactured; not spontaneous.

> That fruit looks nutritious,
> but in fact, it's factitious—
> in other words, fake.
> Look before you take!

hieratic (HI-ur-AT-ik)

adj. highly formal or stylized, as a work of art. Originally: a cursive form of ancient Egyptian writing, less pictorial than hieroglyphic, used in ancient times by Egypt's priestly class.

> An artist's style hieratic
> is not exactly democratic,
> but more formal
> than is normal.

bandelet (BAN-duhl-et)

n. ring-shaped molding at the top of a column (from the French *bandelette*, a small band).

repine (rih-PĪN)

v.i. to be discontented; complain. Also: to long for.

> Repine
> means to whine
> and complain.
> What a pain.

byronic (bī-RAH-nik)

adj. romantic and melancholy (after the 19th-century poet Lord Byron).

> A boy byronic
> is a chronic
> brooder
> and romantic suitor.

cabotinage (KAB-uh-tin-ozh)

n. shameless playing to the audience (after Cabotin, a 17th-century French actor); behavior characteristic of a second-rate actor.

phatic (FAT-ik)

adj. pertaining to words or speech used to express emotion, esp. goodwill, rather than to impart information.

> Phrases automatic
> like "good day" are phatic.
> They make pleasant conversation
> yet convey no information.

châtelaine (SHAT-uh-lān)

n. the mistress of a chateau or large country house.

> The mistress of the chateau
> boasts of her many beaux.
> What a vain
> châtelaine.

castellan (KASS-tuh-lun)

n. the governor or keeper of a castle.

> The castellan:
> in the castle he's the one
> who's the go-to guy
> for arms—or pie.

bawn (BAWN)

n. a fortified enclosure of a castle; a large house. Also: a cattle enclosure.

orthoepy (awr-THŌ-uh-pee)

n. the ordinary pronunciation of words; the study of the pronunciation of words, esp. with respect to their spellings.

phonate (FŌ-nāt)

v.i. to vocalize.

> When you phonate,
> your vocal chords resonate,
> at which point you're bound
> to make a sound.

ablaut (AH-blout)

n. a vowel change, characteristic of Indo-European languages such as English, usually marking some change in meaning or use (as in *sing, sang, sung, song*).

> The ablaut
> is all about
> "ring rang rung,"
> from which good grammar is sprung.

pullulate (PUHL-yuh-lāt)

v.i. to bud; sprout. Also: to teem; swarm with.

seemly (SEEM-lee)

adj. fitting; decorous; in good taste. Also: handsome. *adv.* fittingly; appropriately.

> Something seemly
> is so extremely
> suitable,
> it's indisputable.

Rare WORDS II

appose (uh-PŌZ)

v.t. to put things side by side.

> To appose
> is to put "these" with "those."
> "Near" and "wide"
> go side by side.

ashlar (ASH-lur)

n. a rectangular, cut building stone.

irrefragable (ih-REH-fruh-guh-buhl)

adj. impossible to dispute; undeniable. Also: unbreakable; unalterable.

> The evidence is not negligible;
> in fact, it's irrefragable.
> You cannot refute
> what's beyond dispute.

lippen (LIP-un)

v.i. to trust or rely on (usually used with "to"— e.g., "I lippen to her"). *v.t.* to entrust to.

> The finance folks I lippen to
> would never let me slip into
> a pecuniary ditch—
> they're paid to keep me rich.

kerf (KURF)

n. a notch or incision made by a cutting tool, such as a saw or an ax. Also: the width of a saw's cut.

> I make this kerf
> to delineate my turf.
> Don't move
> beyond this groove.

wainscot (WĀNS-kot)

n. paneling, usually of wood, applied to the walls of a room. Also: the lower part of an interior wall when finished in a material different from that of the upper part.

dulcify (DUHL-sih-FĪ)

v.t. to make sweet or agreeable; mollify; sweeten.

> The dish is fried
> and dulcified
> with sugar and honey—
> so fattening, but so yummy.

postern (PŌ-sturn)

n. a back door or gate.

> It's the ghost's turn
> to use the postern.
> Specters abhor
> using the front door.

refect (rih-FEKT)

v.t. to refresh, esp. with food or drink.

> When I'm tired and dejected,
> I need to be refected
> with drink and food
> to improve my mood.

pyx (PIKS)

n. a small box or coffer. Also: a container for carrying communion wafers.

spatiate (SPAY-shee-ĀT)

v.i. to rove; ramble.

> A spacy date
> will spatiate,
> making bad impressions
> with his digressions.

judder (JUD-ur)

n. a violent shudder or shaking. *v.i.* to vibrate violently.

> Judder
> is a violent shudder:
> a shake
> like an earthquake.

concatenation (kun-kat-ih-NAY-shun)

n. a chain of events or linked things.

> History says our nation
> was formed by a concatenation
> of revolutions
> and their evolutions.

conterminous (kun-TUR-min-uss)

adj. sharing boundaries; within a common boundary. Also: having the same scope or extent in time.

eagre (EE-gur)

n. a high tidal wave caused by the rushing of the tide up a narrowing estuary; a flood tide.

> The story of Noah
> just goes to show, a
> boat can't be meager
> to survive an eagre.

degust (dih-GUST)

v.t. to taste carefully; savor (from the same root as gusto).

> One with food-lust
> likes to degust
> and savor
> every flavor.

scupper (SKUP-ur)

v.t. to ruin; wreck; destroy. Also: to overwhelm militarily or massacre. *n.* an opening permitting water to drain from a ship's deck.

> Why do you scupper
> my plans to make supper?
> Don't you think my dishes
> are delicious?

inchoate (in-KŌ-it)

adj. just coming into being; incipient; not yet developed; imperfectly developed.

> You want to see a
> good idea?
> I'd love to show it,
> but it's too inchoate.

repugn (rih-PYOON)

v.t. to oppose or refute; contest.

> Repugn
> that goon.
> Refute him!
> It'll suit him.

monticle (MON-tik-ul)

n. a small mountain or hill; hillock.

Rare WORDS II

phrenic (FREN-nik)

adj. pertaining to the mind. Also: anatomically, pertaining to the diaphragm.

> A writer Hellenic
> on matters phrenic
> was Aristotle,
> the Great Alexander's model.

shim (SHIM)

n. a thin, tapered piece of wood or other material for adjusting or leveling heavy items, or filling in spaces between parts subject to wear.

moiety (MOI-ih-tee)

n. a half. Also: a portion or share.

dunnage (DUN-ij)

n. loose material placed under or around cargo to protect it from damage during shipping.

> A ship with large tonnage
> uses tons of dunnage
> to prevent cargo from shaking
> and subsequently breaking.

dispendious (dih-SPEN-dee-us)

adj. expensive; costly; extravagant.

> We buy things dispendious
> so everyone will envy us:
> caviar with blinis
> and luxurious Lamborghinis.

thuriferous (thur-IF-er-us)

adj. carrying or producing frankincense.

> Mary to the kings thuriferous
> said, "I see you've brought a gift for us."
> Frankincense it was they bore
> in that nativity scene of yore.

fulvous (FUHL-vuss)

adj. tawny; dull yellowish-brown or yellowish-gray.

epicene (EP-ih-seen)

adj. having characteristics of both sexes.

> Don't call the epicene
> obscene;
> it's just a gender
> bender.

asyndeton (uh-SIN-dih-TON)

n. the omission of conjunctions, such as "and" and "but," for rhetorical effect.

> "We'll have drinks, laughs, fun 'til dawn"
> is an example of asyndeton.
> In the case at hand,
> we're missing an "and."

viduated (VID-yoo-ay-tid)

adj. left widowed, desolate or destitute.

> The woman viduated
> finds herself situated
> without husband, money or land.
> Fate has played her a cruel hand.

ataraxy (AT-uh-RAK-see)

n. freedom from mental disturbance or emotional disquiet; stoical indifference; imperturbability.

laches (LACH-iz)

n., n.pl. negligence in timely assertion of some right, resulting in the loss of the right.

> The doctrine of laches
> in good time catches
> you if you procrastinate:
> you lose your rights if you're late.

stirps (STURPS)
stirpes (STUR-peez)

n., *n.pl.* a line of descendants, or the person from whom a family line is descended.

> Queen Liz thought Mary Queen of Scots
> a perp,
> the kind who usurps
> a monarch's throne,
> so to the executioner's block she was shown.
> (Liz was succeeded by Mary's stirps.)

fleer (FLEER)

v.t. to laugh at in derision or contempt. *v.i.* to grin or smirk contemptuously. *n.* a jeering or jibe.

> To fleer
> is to jeer.
> I prefer good vibes
> to unkind jibes.

jape (JĀP)

v.t. to jest at; make fun of. *v.i.* to speak mockingly. *n.* a jest.

> Don't jape
> an ape.
> His sense of humor
> is a simian rumor.

ecdysis (EK-duh-SISS)

n. the act of stripping. Originally: the act of shedding an outer coat or outer layer of skin; molting.

endysis (EN-duh-SISS)

n. the development of a new coat of hair, set of feathers, scales, etc.

sough (SOU)

v.t. to make a soft sighing or murmuring sound.
n. an example of this sound. Also: a drainage
ditch; sewer.

> Stand at the ship's bow
> to hear the gentle sough
> made by wind and sea—
> such music to me.

flagitious (fluh-JISH-uss)

adj. egregiously villainous; vicious (can refer to a
person, an act, a crime or a time period).

> Flagitious
> means evil and vicious.
> It can refer to killin'
> or a scandalous villain.

prolepsis (prō-LEP-siss)
prolepses (prō-LEP-seez)

n., n.pl. rhetorical anticipation of a future event—
e.g., "If you tell the cops, you're a dead man."
Also: anticipation of possible objections to an
argument before they are made.

Brahman (BRAH-mun)

n. a member of a social or cultural elite. Also: a member of a superior, priestly caste among Hindus.

> A Brahman
> is of a caste not common,
> although some wish caste
> were a thing of the past.

princeps (PRIN-seps)
principes (PRIN-suh-peez)

n., n.pl. the chief of a district, tribe or community (from the Latin, "first person"; Caesar Augustus and his successors assumed the title for its associations with republicanism, but eventually it acquired autocratic connotations).

apotropaic (ap-uh-trō-PAY-ik)

adj. intended to avert bad luck; reputed to ward off evil.

> To avoid getting stuck
> with a run of bad luck,
> some use rites apotropaic,
> now considered archaic.

malefic (muh-LEH-fik)

adj. doing or producing evil; having a malignant influence.

> Malefic
> means terrific
> at doing harm,
> like a bad-luck charm.

dysphoria (diss-FAWR-ee-uh)

n. a state of mental discomfort or unease; the opposite of euphoria.

splenetic (splih-NET-ik)

adj. irritable; testy (after the spleen, the organ believed in medieval medicine to be responsible for ill temper). Also: melancholy.

> The mom made efforts frenetic
> to soothe the babe splenetic.
> Though she clucked and cooed,
> the child frowned and boo-hoo'd.

relegable (REH-lih-guh-buhl)

adj. capable of being exiled or banished. Also: capable of being referred to an inferior position, place or condition.

> One who's relegable
> is eligible
> for banishing,
> if not vanishing.

perforce (pur-FAWRSS)

adv. necessarily; as the result of circumstance.

> Dorothy had no alternate course,
> so she perforce
> took the Yellow Brick Road
> to the Wizard's abode.

scrabble (SKRA-buhl)

v.t., v.i. to scratch about hurriedly with the hands, claws or feet. Also: to struggle, as if by scraping or scratching.

restive (RESS-tiv)

adj. impatient under correction, direction or rules; unwilling to be controlled or directed. Also: stubborn; refusing to move; obstinate.

> If you a math test give,
> I will get restive.
> Every digit
> makes me fidget.

quiescent (kwee-ESS-unt)

adj. at rest; quiet; still.

> I prefer a sea quiescent
> to the incessant
> motion
> of a restless ocean.

wayworn (WAY-worn)

adj. worn out or tired by traveling.

benthos (BEN-thoss)

n. the bottom of a sea, lake or ocean. Also: all organisms living on the bottom of a body of water.

> Careless men toss
> their litter in the water.
> It lands in the benthos.
> Be more careful, they oughter.

thalassic (thuh-LASS-ik)

adj. pertaining to the sea, esp. inland seas.

> A book thalassic
> that's a classic
> is *Moby-Dick*—
> a read that's not quick.

oe (Ō)

n. a small island.

> Land ho!
> An oe!
> An isle
> smaller than a square mile!

resipiscence (rih-SIP-ih-sinss)

n. repentance or remorse resulting from harsh experience.

> His eloquence
> convinced me that his resipiscence
> was real;
> he was sorry that he tried to steal.

anodyne (AN-uh-dīn)

n. a medicine that soothes pain or the mind. *adj.* assuaging pain or soothing the mind. Also: bland; inoffensive.

> An anodyne
> relieves body or mind
> and causes pain
> to wane.

kahuna (kuh-HOO-nuh)

n. a Hawaiian medicine man or shaman. Also: an important or prominent person.

> Soon a
> kahuna
> will heal
> the pain you feel.

saccadic (suh-KAH-dik)

adj. twitching; jerky. Also: the rapid, jerky movement of the eyes as they fix on one point after another.

> Your movements saccadic
> can appear psychotic.
> Here's a switch:
> Ditch the twitch.

nystagmus (nih-STAG-muss)

n. rapid, involuntary, side-to-side movement of the eyeballs.

propense (prō-PENSS)

adj. leaning or inclining toward; prone to; disposed.

Rare WORDS II

When a man is to something propense,
he is getting off the fence:
he may not yet have made up his mind,
but in a certain direction he is inclined.

tropism (TRŌ-piz-um)

n. the turning of an organism toward or from a stimulus, such as light, heat or gravity.

nuncupative (NUN-kyuh-PAY-tiv)

adj. made orally (esp. of a will); not written.

Don't let your mate give
you a will nuncupative.
You'll get bitten
with last wishes unwritten.

battology (buh-TOL-uh-jee)

n. unnecessary or tiresome repetition in speaking or writing.

An apology, apology
for my battology, battology,
and contrition, contrition
for my needless repetition.

putative (PYOO-tuh-tiv)

adj. supposed; reputed; commonly thought or deemed.

stasis (STAY-siss)

n. equilibrium; motionlessness. Also: stagnation.

Stay, Sis,
in stasis:
Stay still
if you will.

mesial (MEE-zee-uhl)

adj. in or near the middle.

ligature (LIG-uh-chur)

n. the act of binding; something used for binding—
e.g., a thread or string for binding an artery.

> That artery's so big, I'm sure
> even a blind doc could find it
> and use a ligature
> to bind it.

rete (REE-tee)

retia (REE-tee-uh)

n., n.pl. a network, esp. of veins, arteries or nerves.

> Too much that's meaty
> could clog an arterial rete.
> Rather than buy it,
> go on a diet.

botryoid (BAH-tree-oid)

adj. shaped like a grape cluster.

rhizoid (RĪ-zoid)

n. a delicate, root-like structure by which mosses
and ferns attach themselves to the material in
which they grow. *adj.* root-like; filament-like.

abscission (ab-SIZH-un)

n. the act of cutting off. Also: the natural breaking
away of leaves, flowers and fruit from a plant.

> An abscission
> with precision
> requires no wizards—
> use scissors.

gestalt (gesh-TAHLT)

n. a whole that cannot be determined from
the parts.

> A thing is more than the sum of its parts,
> but seeing that thing is an art.

Rare WORDS II

> Grasping the gestalt
> is what it's all about.

autochthonous (aw-TOK-thuh-nuss)

adj. indigenous; originating where found; native to the place inhabited.

> If this plague upon us
> is autochthonous,
> it's native to our region.
> Let's move—such plagues are legion.

obsidian (ob-SID-ee-un)

n. a hard, dark, volcanic glass. *adj.* glassy and black, like obsidian.

furcate (FUR-kāt)

adj. forked; branching. *v.i.* to form a fork; branch.

> Only a dork
> would eat soup with a fork.
> Save this furcate device
> for veggies or rice.

sorites (suh-RĪ-teez)

n. an argument formed by several smaller arguments, the conclusion of each forming the premise of the next (ult. from the Greek *soros*, heap). A sorites can sometimes lead to an erroneous conclusion, as in the original sorites argument: One grain of sand does not make a heap. Adding one additional grain does not make it a heap. Adding another does not make it a heap. Thus, no additional amount of sand will make it a heap.

> Add one grain,
> then another, in vain—
> no amount of sand will form a heap.
> That's a sorites leap.

qat (KAHT)

n. a shrub cultivated in the Middle East and Africa for its leaves and buds, which are the source of a euphoric stimulant when chewed or used as a tea.

wadi (WAH-dee)

n. a dry valley that becomes a water channel during the rainy season, found in northern Africa and southwest Asia (from the Arabic).

> Beam me up, Scotty—
> I'm stuck in a wadi,
> and I shiver
> to think it could become a river.

vail (VĀL)

v.t., v.i. to let sink or lower. Also: to doff one's hat.

vail (VĀL)

v.t., v.i. to be of use or profit; avail.

> I'll vail my hat to respect you
> if it avails me not to reject you.
> Manners fail me
> when it doesn't vail me.

rheme (REEM)

n. in linguistics, the part of a sentence that comments on a topic (e.g., in the sentence

"As for me, I love apples," "me" is the topic, and "I love apples" is the rheme).

> A rheme
> is a comment on a theme.
> (That's a take simplistic
> on this term linguistic.)

syllepsis (sih-LEP-siss)

n. a construction in which a word governs two or more words, but agrees in number, gender, case or application with only one of the words.

> "I met my fate and step-sis"
> is a syllepsis.
> The word "met" has two leanings,
> and the sentence employs both meanings.

accidence (AK-sih-dunss)

n. the rudiments or essentials of a subject, esp. grammar.

expatiate (iks-PAY-shee-ĀT)

v.i. to speak or write at length. Also: to wander about.

> One does not ingratiate
> when one expatiates.
> Few have the strength
> to listen at length.

meiosis (mī-Ō-siss)

n. understatement for rhetorical effect.

> "Jail ain't no bed of roses"
> is an example of meiosis:
> a statement that understates
> that which is the case.

crocket (KROK-it)

n. a small projecting ornament, usually in the shape of buds, leaves or animals, that curls into itself, often found on pinnacles, gables and the like in Gothic architecture.

fetor (FEE-tur)

n. a strong, unpleasant odor; stench.

> Wash your feet or
> that fetor
> will repel
> everyone with your smell!

ozostomia (ō-zuh-STŌ-mee-uh)

n. bad breath (ult. from the Greek *ozein,* to smell, and *stoma,* mouth).

> If I suffer ozostomia,
> hold your nose or throw me a
> mint.
> I'll get the hint.

xerostomia (zee-ruh-STŌ-mee-uh)

n. abnormal dryness of the mouth.

yare (YEHR)

adj. quick; agile; nimble.

> A ship that is yare
> is likely to fare
> well in battle
> because it's so agile.

grok (GROK)

v.t. to absorb thoroughly; understand profoundly through intuition or empathy (originally from a fictitious Martian language in Robert A. Heinlein's 1961 science fiction classic *Stranger in a Strange Land*).

crenate (KREE-nāt)

adj. finely scalloped; having a notched or scalloped edge, as a leaf.

attar (AT-ur)

n. a fragrant essential oil or perfume obtained from flowers, esp. roses.

> Attar
> is the matter
> turned by toil
> into rose oil.

gambado (gam-BAY-dō)

n. a leaping movement, esp. one made by a horse.

> A man named Alfredo
> performed a gambado
> when informed that he'd won
> a very large sum.

qua (KWAH)

prep., *adv.* in the capacity or character of; as.

> A rose qua rose is a beautiful flower,
> while a rose qua symbol has amorous power.
> *Voilà!*
> That's how you use the word qua.

slue (SLOO)

v.t., *v.i.* to turn on an axis or turn sharply sideways; swivel.

echt (EKT)

adj. authentic; real; genuine.

> I suspect
> that gem is echt.
> Make no mistake—
> it's no fake.

ultimo (UHL-tih-mō)

adv. in the previous month.

> On the 31st ultimo
> I played the lottery and won some dough.
> Today's the 1st and my cash is gone—
> the last of my jewels I'll have to pawn.

proximo (PROK-sih-mō)

adv. in the next month.

> A month from now,
> we'll use the plow.
> Spring is coming, you know,
> on the 20th proximo.

Bibliography

Print Resources

Bulfinch, Thomas. *Bulfinch's Mythology*. New York: Modern Library, 1993.

Calasibetta, Charlotte Mankey. *Fairchild's Dictionary of Fashion*. 2nd rev. ed. New York: Fairchild Books, 1998.

The Compact Edition of the Oxford English Dictionary. 2 vols. Glasgow, Scotland: Oxford University Press, 1971.

D'Aulaire, Ingrid, and Edgar Parin. *D'Aulaire's Book of Greek Myths*. Garden City, N.Y.: Doubleday, 1962.

Eiseley, Loren. "The Chresmologue." In *The Night Country*. Lincoln, Neb.: University of Nebraska Press, 1997.

———. *Man, Time, and Prophecy*. New York: Harcourt, Brace & World, 1966.

Greenman, Robert. *Words That Make a Difference and How to Use Them in a Masterly Way*. Delray Beach, Fla.: Levenger Press, 2000.

Heifetz, Josefa. *Mrs. Byrne's Dictionary of Unusual, Obscure, and Preposterous Words*. Secaucus, N.J.: University Books, 1974.

Hill, Robert H. *Jarrold's Dictionary of Difficult Words*. New York: Howell, Soskin, 1946.

Jellinek, E. "Thomas Bowdler: Censor, Philanthropist, and Doctor." *The Lancet* 358, no. 9287: 29 (September 2001): 1091-94.

Liddell, H. G., and Robert Scott, eds. *An Intermediate Greek-English Lexicon*. Oxford: Clarendon Press, 1987.

Bibliography

Lynch, Jack, ed. *Samuel Johnson's Dictionary: Selections from the 1755 Work That Defined the English Language*. Delray Beach, Fla.: Levenger Press, 2002.

Maher, Kevin. "Shock Revelation: Why Spider-Man's Name Isn't Peter Parkour." *The Times (London)*. 26 April 2007, sec. Times2, p. 20.

Milton Bradley Company. *The Official Scrabble Players Dictionary: Third Edition*. Springfield, Mass.: Merriam-Webster, 1996.

Naylor, Paul Kenneth. "The Pre-Position 'Of': Being, Seeing, and Knowing in George Oppen's Poetry." *Contemporary Literature* 32 no. 1 (Spring 1991): 100-15.

The New Shorter Oxford English Dictionary: The New Authority on the English Language. 2 vols. Edited by Lesley Brown. Oxford: Clarendon Press, 1993.

Norback, Craig, and Peter Norback. *Merit Presents the "Must" Words: A Collection of 6,000 Essential Words to Help You Enrich Your Vocabulary*. N.p.: Merit, 1979.

Shakespeare, William. *The Complete Works*. London: Michael O'Mara Books, 1988.

Weekley, Ernest. *An Etymological Dictionary of English*. 2 vols. New York: Dover, 1967.

Wilkinson, Alec. "No Obstacles; Navigating the World by Leaps and Bounds." *The New Yorker* 83 no. 8 (April 16, 2007): 106-16.

Wood, Clement. *Poets' Handbook*. New York: Greenberg, 1940.

Internet Resources

Dates refer to the authors' most recent access before the book's publication.

Aesop. *Aesop's Fables: The Online Collection*. Compiled by John R. Long. 13 October 2007 <http://aesop fables.com>.

Bibliography

AlphaDictionary. Lexiteria. 13 October 2007
  <http://www.alphadictionary.com>.

*The American Heritage Dictionary of the English
  Language: Fourth Edition*. Houghton Mifflin.
  9 October 2007 <http://www.bartleby.com/61>.

Ancient Egypt: Writing. The British Museum. 13 October
  2007 <http://www.ancientegypt.co.uk/writing/home.
  html>.

Bartleby.com: Great Books Online. Edited by Steven H.
  van Leeuwen. 13 October 2007 <http://www.bartleby.
  com>.

Bentley, Edmund Clerihew. *Selected Works: Clerihews
  from "Biography for Beginners."* Poets' Corner.
  13 October 2007 <http://www.theotherpages.org/
  poems/bentley1.html>.

Britannica Concise Encyclopedia. Encyclopædia
  Britannica. 13 October 2007 <http://www.answers.
  com/library/Britannica%20Concise%20Encyclopedia>.

Chrisomalis, Steven. *Forthright's Phrontistery:
  International House of Logorrhea, The Word List*.
  13 October 2007 <http://phrontistery.info>.

Columbia Encyclopedia. Columbia University Press. 13
  October 2007 <http://www.bartleby.com/65>.

Crane, Gregory R., ed. *The Perseus Project*. Tufts
  University. 13 October 2007 <http://www.perseus.
  tufts.edu>.

Dictionary.com Unabridged. vol 1.1. Random House. 13
  October 2007 <http://dictionary.reference.com/help/
  luna.html>.

Dictionary.com/Word of the Day. Lexico Publishing Group.
  8 October 2007 <http://www.dictionary.com/
  wordoftheday/archive>.

Donovan, Stephen M. *The Catholic Encyclopedia*.
  Vol. 5, 1909. Transcribed by Christine J. Murray.
  New Advent. 13 October 2007 <http://www.
  newadvent.org/cathen>.

Bibliography

Easton's 1897 Bible Dictionary. Thomas Nelson.
13 October 2007 <http://www.ccel.org/ccel/easton/
ebd2.EBD.html>.

Encyclopædia Britannica. Encyclopædia Britannica
Online Library Edition 2007. 13 October 2007
<http://library.eb.com>.

Garg, Anu, ed. *A.Word.A.Day*. 13 October 2007
<http://wordsmith.org/awad/archives.html>.

Harper, Douglas. *Online Etymology Dictionary*.
13 October 2007 <http://www.etymonline.com>.

Hum110 Iliad Homepage. Reed University. 13 October
2007 <http://academic.reed.edu/humanities/110Tech/
Iliad.html>.

Languagehat. 13 October 2007 <http://www.languagehat.
com>.

The 'Lectric Law Library. 13 October 2007 <http://www.
lectlaw.com>.

LoveToKnow Free Online Encyclopedia. Based on the 11th
edition of the Encyclopaedia Britannica, 1911.
LoveToKnow. 13 October 2007 <http://www.1911
encyclopedia.org>.

Merriam-Webster's Dictionary of Law. Merriam-Webster.
13 October 2007 <http://dictionary.reference.com/
help/mwlaw.html>.

OED Online. Edited by John Simpson. Oxford
University Press. 13 October 2007 <http://www.oed.
com>.

On-line Medical Dictionary. Academic Medical
Publishing & CancerWEB. 8 October 2007
<http://cancerweb.ncl.ac.uk/omd/index.html>.

Quinion, Michael. *World Wide Words: Weird Words*.
13 October 2007 <http://www.worldwidewords.org/
weirdwords>.

Bibliography

Silva Rhetoricae. 13 October 2007 <http://rhetoric.byu. edu>.

Spencer, Priscilla. *What's In a Name? The Guide to Harry Potter Name Etymology.* 13 October 2007 <http://www.theninemuses.net/hp/4.html>.

Stanford Encyclopedia of Philosophy. Edited by Edward N. Zalta. Stanford University. 13 October 2007 <http://plato.stanford.edu>.

Stoddard, Samuel. *Fun with Words: A Celebration of the English Language*. A Rinkworks production. 13 October 2007 <http://www.rinkworks.com/ words>.

Taylor, Alan. *Luciferous Logolepsy: Dragging Obscure Words into the Light of Day*. 8 October 2007 <http://www.kokogiak.com/logolepsy>.

Verse Forms: Light Verse Resource Center. Doggerel Daze. 13 October 2007 <http://www.ddaze.com/04LV Resource/Forms.htm>.

Webster's New Millennium Dictionary of English, Preview Edition. Vol. 0.9.7. Edited by Barbara Ann Kipfer. Lexico Publishing Group. 13 October 2007 <http://dictionary.reference.com/wnmde>.

Webster's Revised Unabridged Dictionary, 1913. Micra. 13 October 2007 <http://dictionary.reference.com/ help/web1913.html>.

Webster's Third New International Dictionary, Unabridged. Merriam-Webster. 13 October 2007 <http://unabridged. merriam-webster.com>.

Word Spy: Words About Words. Paul McFedries and Logophilia Ltd. 7 November 2007 <http://www. wordspy.com/waw>.

WordNet 1.6. Princeton University. 13 October 2007 <http://wordnet.princeton.edu>.

Acknowledgments

First and foremost, perfervid thanks to Dana Lynne Singfield for her editorial moil, her rarihew contributions, her titivations and afflatus—she's the greatest.

"Peer reviewer" is a misnomer for James Girsch, since he is peerless as a lexicographer. We have been honored to have Jaimie's guidance as a scholar of Medieval Latin, former associate editor of the *Middle English Dictionary,* etymology review editor for the *Encarta World English Dictionary* and senior editor of the *Thorndike Barnhart Dictionary Series.*

Our book is immeasurably better because of the remarkable eye and impeccable research of David Pierce at Middle East Technical University in Ankara. Bill Fant does a splendid job of running the J-list, where Steve Thomas, Owen Goldin, Lisa Eckstrom, Weldon Goree, Brian McGuire, Lee Mendelson, Helene Lovenheim, Benjamin Bloom and Luis Alejandro Salas answered queries about qua and other quandaries.

We would never have encountered the clerihew if it weren't for Mark Fabi. Kaylan Scagliola gave us two rare words: subluxate and her surname. Paul Saffo provided invaluable research on chresmologues.

We send warm wishes to Wendie Myles, the Weiners, the Lucases, the Mansons, the Cobb-Waggoners, the Frankels, Gertie Marotta, Maxine Cheson and all other emes and aunts and their stirpes. "Tiregroove"—to use Ross Leighton's hypocoristic—provided considerable technical assistance. Thanks to Tanya Cawthorne, Rita Bernard Easton, Nir Goona, Andorra Hodgin, Malvin Lindner, Julie Marron, Heather Sue Mercer, Chaim Morgulis and Nena Sepulveda for their sodality. We are much obliged to authors Fran Lebowitz and William Kowalski for their *bons mots.*

Acknowledgments

Hallie is indebted to Stephen M. Adler and his exemplary staff at the eleemosynary Charity Brands Marketing. If she groks half of the knowledge in Ira Szot's encephalon, she will be wise indeed.

We are grateful to Steve and Lori Leveen for giving the *Rare Words* series such a beautiful home at Levenger. We believe that the caliber of the Levenger catalog is a major reason for the book's success. We are especially fortunate to have a *belle esprit* like Mim Harrison to edit *Rare Words II*; her discernment and attentiveness to detail have yet again been indispensable. The design of Danielle Furci's and the lovely-limned drawings by Marina de Conciliis make the book a visual delight. Thanks also to the other members of the Levenger Press gang—Ray Moore, Vicki Ehrenman, Tina St. Pierre and Tim Barbini.

The rarest of words could not describe our warm thoughts for Lynda Myles and James Pendleton, both distinguished authors and playwrights and amazing people. Their dedication to the craft of writing and way with words have been an inspiration to us in the writing of this book.

Index of Words

Index of Words

Index of Words

endogamy 17
endysis 95
engagé 37
ensiform 84
ensorcell 70
enteron 76
ephectic 41
epicene 94
epigamic 20
epoche 42
eruct 48
euonym 21
ewer 16
excursus 14
exogamy 17
expatiate 105

F

fabulist 22
facetiae 83
facies 15
factitious 86
farrago 63
farrier 42
farrow 48
fatidic 45
favonian 33
febricity 80
feckless 19
fetor 106
fillip 49
flagitious 96
fleer 95
flummery 28
foramen 41
fordo 40
foudroyant 32
froward 37
fugle 45
fulvous 94
funambulist 44
furcate 103

G

gadroon 78
gambado 107
gambol 79
genesic 48
gestalt 102
glossolalia 16
gnathal 59
gramineous 78
gratulate 44
gravic 73
gravid 42
grok 106
grume 47
guerdon 77
gynecic 49
gyre 80

H

habiliments 29
haboob 34
halidom 23
halieutics 30
handsel 36
haver 61
helpmeet 82
hieratic 86
hircine 15
hirsute 22
hydrargyrum 79
hypocoristic 21

I

icarian 35
illusor 41
imbricate 55
impasto 85
imprecate 35
impresa 69
inchmeal 13
inchoate 92

Index of Words

Index of Words

Index of Words

recondite 67
recrudescent 70
redivivus 13
redound 19
reductio ad absurdum 38
refect 90
regulus 14
relegable 98
reliquiae 53
repand 50
repine 86
repugn 92
resipiscence 99
restive 98
rete 102
rheme 104
rhizoid 102
riparian 30
rodomontade 25
roister 28
rupicolous 51
rustication 43
ruttish 23

S

saccadic 100
saltimbanco 47
salvific 64
samizdat 73
sanative 77
saprogenic 54
scagliola 85
scandent 53
scapular 80
sclerous 41
scrabble 98
scrutator 83
scrutoire 76
scumble 72
scupper 92
scutwork 31
sectary 70

seemly 88
selcouth 43
selenian 20
sematic 86
seminal 27
senary 71
seraphic 23
servitor 36
sessile 79
shim 93
shivaree 27
sidereal 20
sigmoid 26
singultus 35
skift 33
slue 108
sodality 82
solmization 36
somatic 59
sorites 103
sortilege 70
sough 96
spatiate 91
splenetic 98
stasis 101
stipple 72
stirps 95
stramineous 47
subluxate 83
suborn 66
subsume 24
subulate 26
sulcate 51
sumptuary 51
sural 44
surd 73
swain 43
sweal 69
syllepsis 105
sylvatic 43
syncretism 40

Index of Words

T

tautology 33
tergiversate 18
tesselate 14
testudinal 80
thalassic 99
theandric 45
theodolite 56
thrasonic 25
thuriferous 93
tiffin 84
titivate 31
touchstone 51
traceur 68
transom 34
trichotillomania 49
trochal 80
tropism 101
trumpery 29
tuckahoe 66
tyrosis 61

U

ultimo 108
ungulate 42
unregenerate 37
ursine 15

V

vail 104
vendition 52
verecund 13
veriest 41
verism 40
vernissage 85
vestal 22
viands 85
viaticum 62
viduated 94
visile 16
viviparous 62
vug 51

W

wadi 104
wainscot 89
wayworn 99
weltanschauung 24
weltschmertz 24

X

xerostomia 106

Y

yare 106
yisser 60

About the Authors

Raised in a multilingual household, Jan Leighton was propense to rare words from early childhood. He collected words during his Air Force tour of Europe (*cicerone*) and North Africa (*haboob*), his music studies at the University of Mexico (*solmization*) and his classes in stage directing with Lee Strasburg (where cabotinage was verboten). He graduated from the American Theater Wing in New York City (where he learned about *ka* from Joe Anthony).

Mr. Leighton has portrayed more than 3,000 historical personages, including several mentioned in this book: Aristotle, Shakespeare, Henry Fielding, Julius Caesar, Captain Ahab (*Moby-Dick*) and Merlin.

Hallie Leighton, his daughter, is a graduate of the High School of Performing Arts; several dramatic monologues of hers were published in a compilation, *Sometimes I Wake Up in the Middle of the Night*. At St. John's College in Annapolis, Maryland, and Santa Fe, New Mexico, she learned Euclid's *reductiones ad absurdum* and ancient Greek as part of her studies of the Great Books of the Western World.

After receiving a Bachelor of Arts in the college's classical liberal arts program, Ms. Leighton worked in publishing, at Random House and Knopf, and in television. Her clerihews have been published in *Slate*. She was recently a writer-in-residence in the Arad Arts Project in Arad, Israel, where she learned Hebrew and wrote about Jewish-Bedouin relations. She currently works in marketing, developing strategic partnerships between corporations and nonprofit organizations.

The Leightons live in Manhattan.

Uncommon Books
for Serious Readers

A Boy at the Hogarth Press
Written and illustrated by
Richard Kennedy

Delight
J. B. Priestley

The Dream
Sir Winston Churchill

Feeding the Mind
Lewis Carroll

A Fortnight in the Wilderness
Alexis de Tocqueville

**The Little Guide to
Your Well-Read Life**
Steve Leveen

The Making of The Finest Hour
Speech by Winston S. Churchill
Introduction by Richard M. Langworth

More Words That Make a Difference
with passages from
The Atlantic Monthly
Robert Greenman and Carol Greenman

Notes on Our Times
E.B. White

On a Life Well Spent
Cicero
Preface by Benjamin Franklin

Rare Words
Jan Leighton
and Hallie Leighton

Samuel Johnson's Dictionary
Edited by Jack Lynch

Samuel Johnson's Insults
Edited by Jack Lynch

The Silverado Squatters
Six selected chapters
Robert Louis Stevenson

Spoken Like a Pro
Mim Harrison

Words That Make a Difference
with passages from
The New York Times
Robert Greenman

Levenger Press is the publishing arm of

LEVENGER®
TOOLS FOR SERIOUS READERS

www.Levengerpress.com   800.544.0880